THE

Secret

OF

CHRISTIAN
LIVING

THE

Secret

OF

CHRISTIAN
LIVING

WATCHMAN NEE

CHRISTIAN FELLOWSHIP PUBLISHERS, INC
NEW YORK

THE SECRET OF CHRISTIAN LIVING

ISBN 13: 978-0-935008-88-3
ISBN 10: 0-935008-88-8

Available from the Publishers at:

11515 Allecingie Parkway
Richmond, Virginia 23235
www.c-f-p.com

Printed in the United States of America

FOREWORD

The consuming desire of all true Christians is to be like Christ Jesus. Without doubt, such holy ambition is inspired by the Holy Spirit. For it is God's eternal will that all who are called by Him are to be conformed to the image of His beloved Son. Yet how ironical it is that most Christians seem to undergo great frustration in failing to reach that goal. Does God plan it that way or do we fail to know and appropriate the provision of God? Thank God, He never calls without providing. Therefore, it behooves us to enter into the secret of Christian living.

Truth is always simple in nature. This entire secret of Christian living is given in two simple phrases, which are: "in Christ" and "Christ in us."

In this present volume, brother Watchman Nee presents the secret of Christian living in three parts; namely, in Christ, Christ in us, and some applications. These are messages given mainly from 1934 to 1938 in various cities of China. They are more direct, more illustrative and easier to understand. It can be viewed as a companion volume to the classic, *The Normal Christian Life.*[*]

---

[*] Watchman Nee, *The Normal Christian Life* (Tyndale, Christian Literature Crusade). Still available.

THE SECRET OF CHRISTIAN LIVING

A companion volume to *The Normal Christian Life*

Part One:
In Christ

Chapter 1

IN CHRIST

"Of him [God] are ye in Christ Jesus" (1 Cor. 1.30a).

"Blessed be the God and Father of our Lord Jesus Christ, who hath blessed us with every spiritual blessing in the heavenly places in Christ" (Eph. 1.3).

The phrase "in Christ" is most simple, yet its meaning is very deep. For there will be no gospel if there is no "in Christ." Neither will there be the church if there is no "in Christ." Without "in Christ," there will be no Christianity, neither redemption nor salvation. For whatever God does, He does it in Christ, not in man. All which God does in us, He does in Christ.

Ephesians 1.3 says God "hath blessed us with every spiritual blessing in the heavenly places in Christ." "Every" can also be translated as "all." As we read this verse, we may consider God's word as redundant and hence wearisome. It seems unnecessary to add "in Christ" to "spiritual blessing in the heavenly places." Why is the word of God phrased in such a way? Should we understand this, we would know without doubt what Christianity is. We would know the plan of God's redemption work as well as the way God works. For in God's redemptive plan, He does not deal directly with man. The Bible shows us that God's way of dealing with mankind is not on the basis of individuals but is rather on a corporate or collective basis. God does not ask how many sins you have committed, or how many bad things you have done. He only questions you if you are in Adam. Man often pays attention to personal sins, but God includes all mankind in one person who is in Adam. For in that one man you can see yourself. If he has no problem, then neither have you any problem. If he is questionable, so you are questionable.

Only Two Men

According to Biblical principle, there are but two men in the world. It is written in the Scriptures, Adam is the first man. He is

3

called the first man Adam. Christ is the second man, and He is called the last Adam (see 1 Cor. 15.45). Some people may ask, "How do you account for the many men between them? It is evident that there are many, many men in the world. How, then, can you say there are just two men?" This is because in the eyes of God all mankind is included in these two men. Besides these two, there is not a third man, nor any other man. And hence, you are either in Adam or in Christ. Adam would seem, therefore, to be an incredibly big man, in that when you come out of your mother's womb you exist in that big Adam. But when you believe in the Lord and are being born again, you are immediately being translated into Christ.

In Adam

Once I saw a picture in which a woman was wearing a huge apron under which were hidden many children. This is exactly the way God looks at mankind. All men live in Adam. God gathers all men in Adam. We trace the children back to their parents; the parents to the grandparents: one generation after another generation till we reach back to Adam. Thus may we realize that all mankind is in Adam. And hence, whatever Adam did on that long-ago day, we too have done the same thing. When Adam and Eve sinned in the garden of Eden, you and I have sinned likewise. For whatever Adam did, you and I did too.

What is the exact meaning of being "in Adam"? Let me illustrate: When I was in Kaifeng, I was asked by someone to illustrate what is meant by being in Adam. I answered, "The Chinese acknowledge that they come from their ancestor Huang-ti. Once there was a battle between Huang-ti and Si-iu. Suppose during that time, it was not Si-iu who was slain but it was instead Huang-ti. Will there still be the Chinese race?" He answered, "No." "Why should there be no Chinese race if Huang-ti died?" I asked. "Because when Huang-ti died, we also died," he replied. "But Huang-ti can die his death and we can live our lives," I retorted. "Not so," he insisted, "because we all come from Huang-ti, so when Huang-ti died, we too died."

Do you realize that Si-iu does not need to kill each and every one of us. If he could only kill Huang-ti, there will not be any of

4

us remaining, for we are "in Huang-ti." This is how the Scriptures looks at Adam. There is no need for each of us to sin, for as long as we come from Adam we have already sinned. Whatever Adam experienced is our experience. "In Adam all die," says 1 Corinthians 15.22. Adam died, so all died. There is no need to trace your personal history. As long as you are in Adam, whatever Adam passed through is your history too.

In Christ

God uses the same principle to save us. For we are saved in Christ. How did the Lord die for us that we might be saved? Looking from the personal side, I am saved as I believe. But viewing from the corporate side, we have been judged in Christ. For example, let us say that the chalk in a bottle represent so many of us in Christ crucified. I have no need to throw the chalk one by one into the sea. If I merely toss this bottle into the sea, all the chalk will be in the sea as well. For where the bottle is, there is the chalk. Likewise, since we are in Christ, the experience of Christ becomes our experience. When He suffered judgment and death on the cross and as He was raised from among the dead and ascended to heaven, we who are in Him were judged, crucified, resurrected and ascended with Him. Whatever He experienced became our experience. God looks at us as being in Christ, having all the experiences of Christ. This, then, is the redemptive work of God.

How to Be in Christ

Some have asked me how we could be in Christ. My reply was: Suppose I, Nee, who weighs only one hundred and fifty pounds, can put the chalk into the bottle; cannot God who is millions and millions times stronger, put us all in Christ? Please read 1 Corinthians 1.30a: "Of him [God] are ye in Christ Jesus." Who puts us in Christ? It is God. I am in Christ, though I do not know how I am in Christ — just as the chalk does not know how it is in the bottle. Nevertheless, as long as the chalk is placed in the bottle, whatever happens to the bottle happens to the chalk. I do not know how I enter into Christ, but I do know that God has already put me in Christ. As Christ is, so am I. Here we notice one thing: that in God's redemptive work He does not deal with individuals, but with Christ. Today God sets up two camps in the world — the camp of Christ and the camp of Adam. You have the right today to choose to be in Adam or in Christ. If you are in Adam, you die. But if you are in Christ, you get saved. For God will not do anything outside of either Adam or Christ.

There was one who asked, "Do you think I could go to hell?" I said, "You seem to be well qualified." "How could such a good person as I am go to hell?" he retorted. "Because you already have the qualification," I replied. "I do not ask how good or how bad you are. I only ask are you in Christ or in Adam. You do not need to steal, murder, or commit some other serious crime. As long as you are in Adam, you are a candidate for hell."

I recall a wonderful narrative in the Bible. It is recorded in the Epistle to the Hebrews. Hebrews is quite difficult to understand. In order to prove that Christ is more excellent than Moses, Joshua, Aaron and angels, the author of that epistle compares them with Christ. In one of the comparisons he mentions the priesthood of Christ as being more excellent than the priesthood of Aaron. How does he prove his point? He shows that Christ is made priest after the order of Melchizedek whereas Aaron's high priesthood came according to the order of Levi. Aaron had a forefather called Abraham. Once when Abraham returned after a victory in battle, he gave one tenth of his spoil to Melchizedek. Now Aaron came from Levi, Levi from Jacob, Jacob from Isaac, and Isaac from Abraham. When Abraham offered the tithes to Melchizedek, Isaac was in his bowels, and so were Jacob and Levi. Thus, through Abraham, Levi too offered the tithes to Melchizedek. For this reason, the priesthood of Christ which is after the order of Melchizedek is superior to the priesthood of Aaron that was according to the order of Levi.

Every Spiritual Blessing in Christ

Once I had a conversation with a few students majoring in biology. I told them that according to the Bible the age of a father was less than the age of his son. Why could I say so? Because we trace the source of life back to our forefathers. If with the father life has been on earth for six thousand years, and if the son lives to be thirty years old, then by adding thirty to six thousand years, will not the life of the son be longer than his father?

Just as formerly we had the life of Adam, so now we have the life of Christ. When we accepted Adam's life, we became part of Adam. In like manner, as we receive the life of Christ, we become part of Christ. Whatever is in Christ belongs to us. This is the Biblical way of God's salvation.

Here is a problem. Do I need to pursue after these spiritual blessings in Christ? Can I overcome sin without seeking for holiness? Please remember that in order to be holy and perfect, you must look at yourself with the eyesight of God. Forget for the time being the matter of whether you sin or not, of whether you overcome or not. As long as you are in Christ, what you are in yourself does not count. If only you are in the bottle, whatever happens to the bottle happens to you. This is the glad tidings. So we declare that the gospel is free grace. Basically, it does not depend on you. If you are in Christ, then all is yours. For all spiritual blessings in the heavenly places have been given to us in Christ Jesus. There is no way for God not to give all these spiritual blessings to us if we are in Christ. He himself has placed us in Christ; therefore, He cannot withhold any blessing from us. Nothing can be withheld. Christ cannot have ten and we only nine. All which is in Christ has been given to us. Such is God's work. Whether it is salvation, victorious life, power, way, and so forth, all things have been given to us in Christ.

Since God has put you in Christ, and even if you say you are the chief of sinners, you nonetheless have been punished and judged while Christ was punished and judged on the cross. In Christ, all your sins are forgiven. God cannot call them back. For it relates to the grace and righteousness of God. This is what the Epistle to the Romans talks about. There is a time difference between God's grace and God's righteousness. God in Christ reveals the grace of God. What can man do if God has not put him in Christ? That we are in Christ is due to God's grace. But after He puts us in Christ, He has already judged those who are in Christ. Thus our salvation involves not only God's grace but also God's righteousness. Since God has already judged Christ, can He punish us again who are in Christ? Never. After He judged

Christ on the cross, He is obligated to justify us who are in Christ. God is righteous, He cannot but accept what Christ has done.

As Christians, all rests on the fact of our being in Christ. Being in Christ, we enjoy great blessings.

Seeing Christ

Time does not allow me to speak in detail all the things which pertain to our being "in Christ." For in Christ there exist abundant spiritual blessings such as holiness, victory, power, spirituality, faith, spiritual growth, humility, patience, love, and so forth. Whatever spiritual blessings you may think of, they all are in Christ. The problem with Christians today is that they tend to look inward instead of looking outward. If you look inward to yourself for holiness, I can assure you that there is nothing good in yourself. We are prone to forget that when God saved us, He saved us in Christ. We frequently ask ourselves: Now that I am saved, why is my temper still as bad, why am I still so proud, why am I yet so unclean? You long to be victorious, but when you look into yourself, you fail to see patience, humility, holiness, and so forth. On the contrary, you find all kinds of sins such as uncleanness, bad temper, pride, etc. Why? Because you forget that God's way of salvation is in Christ, not in your own self. Patience is in Christ, humility is in Christ, holiness is in Christ. All is in Christ. In you, yourself, there is always uncleanness and unholiness. If you live in Christ, you have everything. But if you live in your self, you remain unchanged.

United with Christ

Never imagine what God has done in you, for you are still as unclean, wicked, unholy and proud as ever. This is because God's grace does not work in you, but only works in Christ. When you are joined to Christ, everything that is in Christ will flow into you; but if you are cast off from Christ, all your own uncleanness will flow back. This is like connecting with a pipe of clean water whereby you get clean water; whereas in connecting with a pipe of dirty water, you only get dirty water.

You imagine that after you are saved, your old Adam will gradually change. But God will now prove to you that there will never be such a thing happening. As long as you are in Adam, you are always unclean. What makes you different is your being in Christ. Only by being in Christ will you be changed. For example: How is a lamp shining? The lamp itself does not give light. It is set aglow when electric current passes through it. Likewise it is with the virtues, the fruit of the Holy Spirit, and the power of God — they are in Christ. By being joined to Christ, the Christian gets everything. Electricity is in the power house. As soon as the lamp is connected to the power house, it gives light. How we habitually say that the lamp gives light. Yet, strictly speaking, it is not the lamp that gives light, rather is it the electric current flowing through the lamp that gives light. The lamp drives away darkness by means of the light of the electricity. In like manner, as long as we are in Christ, connected with Christ, and related to Christ, the power of Christ will flow through us.

I first saw an electric bulb when I was ten years old. I was so surprised to see a dark bulb suddenly brighten up. I removed the bulb after it had given light for two hours and took it in to a dark room, thinking that it would continue to shine. Why was it that as soon as it was removed, it ceased to shine? The reason, of course, is that the bulb itself has no light; it itself is dark. Only as it is in touch with the power house can it immediately shine.

Originally we were all dark. Now that we are in Christ we are able to shine with patience and humility. We tend to forget that such shining is due to our being in Christ. After we have been Christians for a few years, we begin to consider these virtues as ours, not realizing that the moment we leave Christ we have nothing whatsoever.

Of Christ

We are told the following in 1 John 5.11: "the witness is this, that God gave unto us eternal life, and this life is in his Son." God gives eternal life to us in His Son. He has not given us eternal life apart from His Son. Suppose I wrap a piece of iron in a sheet of paper. When I pick up the paper, I simultaneously take up the iron. "He that hath the Son of God hath the life; he that hath not the Son of God hath not the life" (1 John 5.12). Outside of Christ we receive nothing, for nothing is given to us independently. All things are given to us in Christ. If only you could understand and believe this truth, you would have a peaceful rest at night. It is God's doing that we are in Christ, for we can do nothing. All is of Christ, and none is of ourselves. As a consequence of your understanding this, you will give up hope in yourself for any change. The electric bulb cannot give light without electricity. Likewise, you cannot change yourself if today you are cut off from Christ. If there be any change or difference in you, it is not because you yourself have changed, for all is in Christ. Such is the way of God's salvation.[*]

---

[*] Note: Message given at Kulongyu, Oct. 17, 1936.

Chapter 2

IN ADAM OR IN CHRIST

"If any man is in Christ, he is a new creature: the old things are passed away; behold, they are become new" (2 Cor. 5.17).

"Are ye ignorant that all we who were baptized into Christ Jesus were baptized into his death?" (Rom. 6.3)

Inherit in Adam

(1) The Power to Sin

Marvelous is God's way of redemption. Men think of what they must do to be saved, but God does not require us to do anything in order to be saved. For what God does, He does in Christ. While Satan works on Adam, God works in Christ. We need to know one thing before we can understand God's way of salvation. Do you know how a man sins? Do you think he needs to make a decision to sin before he sins? How do you lose your temper? Do you need to consider in the preceding night that you will lose your temper tomorrow? You are too weak tonight to stir up your temper, but you have decided that by tomorrow you will let loose your temper. Of course, there is no such deliberation. For losing one's temper does not require predetermination. It can easily be done without forcing yourself. Sinning is effortless while not to sin demands great strength.

Take light and darkness as an illustration: We have power companies in the world to drive away darkness with light, but we do not have darkness institutions to bring in darkness. We need to purchase light, but darkness arrives without cost. Have you ever bought darkness from a darkness institution? Never. For darkness is natural and it comes effortlessly. Light, on the other hand, requires effort and is costly. In like manner, sinning is easy but not sinning is most difficult.

(2) *Sinning Is Natural*

No one needs to pray or will to sin. To commit sin comes quickly without any preparation. Why is it so? Because sinning is natural to man. To do good is hard for it is unnatural to man. The Bible clearly tells us that all men inherit the nature of Adam, and Adam's nature is a sinful one. "...through one man sin entered into the world" (Rom. 5.12a). Sin enters into the world through Adam. All we who are in Adam have inherited Adam's sinful nature. So, for us to sin is something most natural.

Satan wishes all mankind to sin. He has no time to entice human beings one by one to sin. So what he did was to pour poison into the water source. All who drink this water will die. He put the sin poison in Adam. Adam sinned but all who belong to Adam sin naturally. Today I can repeatedly sin without any effort, without any premeditation or determination. As long as I am related to Adam, I will sin naturally. For Adam's sinful nature and his power to sin has been inherited by us.

(3) *Inherit All in Adam*

Since mankind has such a relationship with Adam, is it at all surprising that all the people in the world sin so naturally? We sin easily. Within two seconds we can burst out in temper. For we have inherited all the power, ideas and plot of sinning from Adam. It is because we are in Adam that we therefore have inherited whatever is in Adam. All which is Adam's has become ours. As we are born of Adam and belong to him, he bequeaths all his properties to us as written in his last will and testament. Hence, we have no need to learn how to sin, because we have already inherited the power of sinning.

The Bible shows us that all which we possess comes from Adam. How does it come to us? Let us illustrate it this way: Suppose you are the father who has earned and accumulated a great sum of money. You have a son born to you, and you love him. You want to bequeath all your money to him. This great sum of money is not earned by your son. It comes from your earning and accumulating. Now you give all your money to your son. This is bequeathing. We may say that Adam passes on to us a lot of "grace," for we gain it without any effort. Just as what

12

Christ gives to us is grace — for all is freely given — so, what sin Adam gives us is also "grace" because we have done nothing to possess it. To all who are born of Adam, he gives them freely the "grace" of sinning. Consequently, we are all sinners. No one needs to learn to sin, for all know how to sin.

We are sinners by birth. We can sin naturally without effort, and we continue to sin. Such is our inheritance in Adam. He causes us to be sinners. He has passed on to us who are in him the power and nature of sin.

Salvation in Christ

(1) Same Principle Works

The way God saves us comes as freely as Adam making us sinners. The principle of God's salvation in Christ is parallel to that of Adam making us sinners. In Adam, you inherit his nature and power of sin without doing anything; so in Christ, you can receive salvation without planning and working for it. For the salvation of God has no other condition except that you must be in Christ. It is freely given to you without any reservation. As long as you are in Christ, everything that belongs to Him is yours. You need not plan for it or work for it. It is a free gift. I sin because I have the life of Adam; I am able to live righteously and holy because now I have the life of Christ in me. I do not have to struggle so long as I abide in Christ.

The gospel overturns our former relationship in Adam. Just as your old relationship in Adam was, so is now your new relationship in Christ. Oh, what amazing grace God has bestowed on us! I can shout with joy, saying, I now can enjoy all which is in Christ! It matters not how strong is the power of Christ or how rich is Christ's possession, we who are in Him can partake and enjoy all of it. And such participation is natural without any effort. Formerly, in Adam we could sin naturally and effortlessly; so now in Christ we are able to be humble, patient, gentle, holy and victorious without straining. As long as you are in Christ you can be all these things, for you have inherited all such ability.

(2) New Creation in Christ

Let us now see what 2 Corinthians 5.17 says: "if any man is in Christ, he is a new creature [or creation]: the old things are passed away; behold, they are become new." It does not say, "if any man does good, he is a new creature." No, the Bible does not put it that way. It does not say that he who wills and labors for good changes from being an old creature to a new creature. Instead, it says: "if any man is *in Christ*, he is a new creature." It does not depend on how you behave in willing or working that you become a new creature. Rather is it that because you are in Christ, you become a new creature. We usually think that by improving ourselves little by little we gradually become a new creature. Perhaps my heart lacks humility, so at least my mouth could first try to be humble; I will learn humility by speaking humbly. Or, first I will learn holiness in my speech and then in my thought. Even though I am unholy, I could gradually change to be holy. Thus one day I will gradually change to be a new creature. It is hard to say how long this will take. Difficult to say, perhaps fast in ten years or slow in twenty years, or unsuccessful through an entire lifetime. But let us read what the word of God says: "if any man is in Christ, he is a new creature." It has nothing to do with what I did. If you are in Christ, you are a new creature.

Once when I was preaching in Kaifeng, I was confronted by the brother of a high official, who said: "You say I have sins, this I agree. But no matter what you say, I am still committed to improve myself through studying Buddhist classics. I have done that for some years. I do not follow the way of the ignorant, for I approach it philosophically. I am seeking for peace in the heart. I acknowledge that the more I study, the more I pursue, the less I am peaceful and tranquil. I have done that for some years. There is not much improvement. So I have decided to spend thirty years in this pursuit, and hopefully I will be successful. According to what you have said, a person can succeed in becoming a new creature in one day if he is in Christ. How can this be? I have read many religious books, and I discover that the way of Christianity is the fastest. But you are so bold in declaring that your way is even faster than that of Christianity. So, tell me what it is." I did not spend time in explaining more, I only asked him to test it. Next day he came to the gospel meeting and told me, "Indeed, your way *is* the fastest. When you have baptism next time, please notify me for I want to be baptized." All who are in Christ become new creatures rapidly. It is not through gradual improvement or slow attainment. All virtues are in Christ. They do not come to the person by self-improvement or human manufacture. If you are in Christ, you possess all these virtues.

Consider again the light bulb as an example. It does not need to pray for long hours and exert much strength to give light. Just let electricity pass through it and it will give light. The bulb does not have light in itself. It simply needs to allow light to go through. So is it with a Christian. He is not dependent on self-improvement or effort to succeed. He only needs to be in touch with Christ, for He is the source of light. Our new birth, holiness, power and all things else are of Christ; none of them is of ourselves. Only in Christ do we possess all these virtues and we can therefore say, "Thanks be to Christ, not to ourselves. Give all the glory to Him, for He has done all and we do nothing. We receive all in Christ." To be in Him is the one and only requisite. There is no other requirement. In Christ you are new creatures and all old things are passed away.

Thus, the overall question is, Are you in Christ or are you in Adam? Sinning or overcoming, perishing or living anew does not depend on you but on which person you are in. Such is God's salvation in the Bible. God saves us by placing us in Christ. As God deals with Christ, He deals with all. Do you remember the illustration of the chalk bottle? Wherever the bottle is, there the chalk is — for it is in the bottle. The destiny of the bottle is the destiny of the chalk. No one needs to be concerned as to the whereabouts of the chalk: he simply inquires where the bottle is. And such is a picture of our relationship to Christ. We are where He is.

(3) In Christ No Condemnation

Let us read two verses of Scripture: "There is therefore now no condemnation to them that are in Christ Jesus. For the law of the Spirit of life in Christ Jesus made me free from the law of sin and of death" (Rom. 8.1-2). These two verses tell us who are not condemned. How often we think that if only we repent, do right and be good, we will not be condemned; but God says that those who are in Christ are not condemned. Our being in Christ is sufficient. Nothing else is needed. There is no other requirement. Why is there no condemnation in Christ? It is because when He was judged on the cross, we all have received judgment in Him. Christ's judgment is our judgment. His experience on the cross becomes our experience. In Christ there is no condemnation. And there is no condemnation the second time. Once Christ was condemned and judged on the cross, He had borne in His body our condemnation and judgment. There cannot be the second condemnation in Adam. Suppose I owe someone one hundred dollars. If I pay it back, the creditor cannot ask for the money anymore. Since we have once received judgment in the cross of Christ, we "now" have no condemnation in Christ.

Though I am tall in stature, yet I am pretty cowardly. In the past I frequently thought what will happen to me if I go to hell. As a matter of fact, I got sick a few times because of the fear of going to hell. Today I am very happy because I believe that God had once judged and punished me in Christ, so now I am in Christ and there is therefore no more condemnation. Thank God, my "IOU" was already paid back by Christ on the cross. God will not again demand payment.

(4) In Christ No Disability

As a debtor is afraid of the creditor, so one who is without debt is fearful of going into debt. We are so weak that we could not but accumulate debts. This is how we feel after we have believed in the Lord. We are fearful lest we sin after we have been forgiven. What should we do? The word "condemnation" in Romans 8.1 in the Greek original has in its meaning two different uses: the official and the civil uses. Officially it carries the meaning of "condemnation," but in civil use the meaning is not "condemnation" but "disability." Hence, this verse may also be translated: "There is therefore now no disability in Christ Jesus." In Adam we have no strength to resist sin, for we are disabled. We have absolutely no resistance to desiring after many sins. We

16

may exercise our will, pray and exert ourselves; yet nothing works. We are always defeated. But now that we are in Christ, we have the power to overcome. Since Christ is almighty, all who are in Him are no longer disabled but have the power. So the issue lies not in how powerful *you* are, it instead depends on whether Christ's power has been passed on to you. In Christ you inherit all that is of Him. Therefore, the issue centers upon whether or not you are in Christ.

(5) *The Law of the Spirit of Life Makes Free*

Why is it that whoever is in Christ has strength and is no longer disabled? The answer is: "For the law of the Spirit of life in Christ Jesus made me free from the law of sin and of death" (v.2). The word "for" demands an antecedent. It explains what has been proposed in verse 1. It gives the reason for what is said in the preceding verse.

In this verse 2 it speaks of "law." What is a law? Law is an unchanging principle. It is something which happens all the time. In China there is a law stating that he who murders must be put to death. This is a law. Whether it is Jack or Jill, he must die if he commits murder. Gravity, too, is a law. Everything that is dropped falls down to earth. No matter if the object is dropped today or is dropped tomorrow, whether it is dropped in Nanjing or in Beijing, it always falls to the ground. For this is what a law is. And here we are told that sin is a law. It means that sin always acts the same way. People always sin. Whoever you are, wherever you go, you will sin. For example: I can lose my temper quickly. If I meet Mr. Cheng, and I get angry, I will get angry with anybody who is like Mr. Cheng. The same temptations get the same reactions: we all will naturally become proud and irritated. When we are faced with the same temptation we will react with pride and irritation. Each time when confronted with the same temptation we will commit the same sin. It seems that we seldom commit new sins. We all appear to possess a certain personal tendency to special sins. That, too, is a law. You are familiar with the sins you have committed. Perhaps you have encountered them for several decades, and each time you sin in the same way. It is really easy for us to sin. Do you know the law of sin? Sin is more than a behavior; it is a law.

This same verse speaks of the law of death. What is death? The scriptural definition of death is extreme disability. Suppose you visit a sick person; you want to say something to comfort him and yet you have no word. This is the law of death. You know you should be holy, righteous and patient, and yet you are unable to be such. This also is the law of death. Each one of us is unconsciously bound by this law of sin and of death. As each time you fall you commit the same sin, so each time what you are not able to do is also the same matter. Perhaps others do not commit the same sins as those you commit or they may be able to do what you cannot do; nevertheless, everyone is under the law of sin and of death.

Here is the way to overcome the law of sin and of death: by the law of the Spirit of life. For the law of the Spirit of life in Christ sets us free from the law of sin and of death. Christ alone is not touched by the law of sin and of death. For instance, I hold in my hand this New Testament. Even though it makes no movement, it nonetheless has the inward tendency of going downward. It does not fall today because there is a counterforce: the power of my three fingers prevents it from falling. Gravity is a force that draws the New Testament down, but my fingers exert a force to oppose its falling. Thus my hand delivers this book from the gravitational force. Just as my hand saves this book (from falling), just so does Christ save us. The Lord uses the Holy Spirit to resist the power of sin. Even though the power of my fingers is small, yet it can counteract the great power of gravity. It is not through the will, strength, expectation or prayer of this book that it does not fall. No, it is my three fingers that prevent its falling. Today we are saved in the same way. Not what we do, but in Christ the law of the Spirit of life delivers us from the law of sin and of death. This is the way we are saved, but so, too, is the way we overcome. All is done in Christ.

All Is in Christ

I thank God, because my salvation, forgiveness, justification, eternal life — all come from Christ and nothing comes from me.

For the Lord declares: "I am... the beginning and the end" (Rev. 22.13). Thank God, He puts me in Christ, who surrounds me. Christ, Christ, all is Christ. We are nothing except what is in Him.[*]

---

[*] Note: Message given at Kulongyu, Oct. 18, 1936.

Chapter 3

IN CHRIST SUBJECTIVELY

"Are ye ignorant that all we who were baptized into Christ Jesus were baptized into his death? We were buried therefore with him through baptism into death: that like as Christ was raised from the dead through the glory of the Father, so we also might walk in newness of life. For if we have become united with him in the likeness of his death, we shall be also in the likeness of his resurrection; knowing this, that our old man was crucified with him, that the body of sin might be done away, that so we should no longer be in bondage to sin; for he that hath died is justified from sin. But if we died with Christ, we believe that we shall also live with him; knowing that Christ being raised from the dead dieth no more; death no more hath dominion over him. For the death that he died, he died unto sin once: but the life that he liveth, he liveth unto God. Even so reckon ye also yourselves to be dead unto sin, but alive unto God in Christ Jesus" (Rom. 6.3-11).

Out of Adam into Christ

How marvelous is the salvation of God. In accomplishing His work of salvation, He has not wrought anything in us; instead, He does practically all His work in Christ. Christ has already accomplished all for us. Now, the only way for us to be saved is to be in Christ. We have no need to ask God to do something in us. So long as we enter into Christ, all which Christ has accomplished becomes effective in us. This, then, is God's salvation. How do we enter into Christ? It is God who places us in Him. In practice, we must first come out of Adam before we can enter into Christ: just as we must first leave the door of one room in order to enter into another. First come out, then go in. First out of Adam, then into Christ.

In Adam by Birth, Out of Adam by Death

Let us consider first how we got into Adam before considering how we get out of Adam. "That which is born of the flesh is flesh; and that which is born of the Spirit is spirit" (John 3.6). Who is in the flesh? He who is born of the flesh. At the time we are born, we are in Adam. The life we receive when we are born of our parents is the life of Adam. Even though we have passed through so many generations, human life is still the life of Adam. We enter into Adam by birth, but we get out of Adam by death. There is no other way. As you die, you terminate your place in Adam. Thank God, He causes us to die to Adam.

While we are in Adam, we cannot avoid sinning. Death is the great emancipation from sin. Death concludes the past. Spiritual things share the same principle as earthly things. "For he that hath died is justified from sin" (Rom. 6.7). After a person has died, he can sin no more. He is freed from sinning. All his will, thought, temper and evils are dead. Once a man in Australia was sentenced to death. The judge gave him one hundred and eighty death sentences because he was so very wicked. Yet once he had died, all such sentences were concluded. Should one have smoked opium, robbed, killed, and committed other crimes — still, once he died, everything ended, for he could no longer sin. Thus, this is the scriptural principle: death ends all.

In Christ We Die

We now know that we enter into Adam by birth and we get out of Adam by death. If we die, we are freed from Adam's sin. The way is clear, but how do we experience it? I was already born in Adam and am a part of Adam. To get out of Adam, I need to die. But how must I die in order to be free of Adam? Can I die by myself? No way. We have no way to die to ourselves. This way of death is prepared by God. If we trust Him, we will die in Christ and get out of Adam. Hallelujah! How precious to be in Christ, for in Christ we may die.

To die in Christ is the work of God. For when Christ died on the cross, God had already placed us in Christ. We died with Him for we were in Him. Once again, let us reuse the parable of the chalk and the bottle. The chalk is in the bottle. If I toss the bottle into the sea, the chalk will also be in the sea. For where the bottle is, there is the chalk. Likewise, God has placed us in Christ. And whatever was the experience of Christ becomes our experience. "Our old man was crucified with him" (Rom. 6.6a). "One died for all, therefore all died" (2 Cor. 5.14b). We died in Christ. Why does God say that if one died, all died? Because all were in Christ. When Christ died, all could not but die. This death did not occur in us; instead, it occurred in Christ.

The Eye of Faith

When I visited Kaifeng the second time, I told people there that we were freed from sin through death. A certain lady said to me: "The Bible says I am dead, but in my daily life I do not seem to be dead. Is there any way that makes me really dead? I know if only I die, I will be freed from sin." So I told her: "In Christ we died. In ourselves we are still alive. As long as you are in Christ, you remain dead. Whenever you live in yourself you are alive. For the death that God has given is in Christ. If you look at yourself, you are not dead. Therefore, you should never see yourself in your own self. You should use the eyes of faith to see yourself dead in Christ. Then you die. God never works in you separately. He works only in Christ. If you remain all the time in Christ, all that He is and accomplishes flows into you."

The light bulb itself does not give light, but when the electric current comes to it, it is set aglow. In ourselves we cannot fail to lose our temper, but in Christ we may naturally be patient.

Some seek death in life, but we find life in death. We must use the eye of faith to see ourselves as being dead in Christ. We in our own selves are not the object of our faith. For the anchor of our faith is Christ. If I, Nee, look within myself, I cannot find death though I have already died in Christ. I do not need to die again. Thank God, in Christ we died. The failure of many Christians lies here. They seek for death in themselves, and they never find it. For when you examine within yourself as to whether you are dead, you continue to live in your own self and are therefore very much alive. Death is in Christ, not in your self.

It is a strange thing that we live in two realms. We were originally in Adam, but now God placed us in Christ. Yet today in actual living we frequently return to Adam. The defeat of many Christians comes from looking within themselves, thus living in their own selves.

There was a sister who was well experienced in the Lord. When people asked her about the secret of Christian living, her answer was: "If you want to experience victorious life and not be defeated, you must never look at yourself outside of Christ. For whenever you see yourself outside of Christ, you will find your former unsaved condition. In looking within yourself, you use your own eyesight and feeling. Only when you look at Christ, you exercise faith and look with God's eye."

The Meaning of Baptism

What must we do once we have died in Christ? The first thing after death is burial. The baptism spoken of in the Bible means burial. One must, of course, die first before he is buried. We bury a person because we believe he is dead. There was once a woman who refused to let people put her husband in the coffin even though he was already dead for three days and three nights. She was afraid that her husband might be suffocated if he were put in a coffin because she did not believe that her husband was truly dead. Will you bury a person if you do not believe he is dead? No, you will not do so. If I am still alive, I will not allow myself to be buried. In baptism you believe in your position in Christ. You believe that you were crucified with Christ. Whatever is of Christ you have a share. Since all who believe in the Son of God are in Christ, they therefore must believe they have died in Christ. If this be true of you, then having such faith, how will you express the reality that you are dead? By being baptized. In baptism you declare that in Christ you died with Him. Through baptism you acknowledge this fact.

We Christians have a "death" that delivers us out of Adam, as well as a "birth" that brings us to Christ. In between this death and birth is a floating bridge which is burial that is expressed through baptism. This enables us to cross from the side of Adam to the side of Christ. For baptism connects Adam to us on the one end and Christ to us on the other. It says farewell to Adam and breaks off all connection with him. It also brings us into Christ and a new beginning in Him.

"In Christ" is the most perfect thought of God to be found in the Bible. Its reality enables us to leave the Adamic realm and join the realm of Christ. In between these two realms is the tomb. After a person dies, the last act is of his being buried. It is the blood which is shed by our Lord that cleanses us of all our sins. Though all the waters in the world will not be able to wash away a single one of our sins, yet the water of baptism testifies that "by death I come out of Adam, but through burial I am able to enter into Christ. I am now in Christ, therefore my sins are cleansed and I am saved."[*]

---

[*] Note: Message given at Kulongyu, Oct. 19, 1936.

Chapter 4

THE BLOOD OF CHRIST

The Double Need of Sinners

Since man had eaten the fruit of the tree of the knowledge of good and evil and was driven out of the garden of Eden, he on the one hand lost the opportunity of receiving God's life directly by which he could have fulfilled the original purpose of God's creation of man, and on the other hand his sinning makes him a sinner. Hence, God must deal not only with the man's sins but also with the man himself. God first sent Christ to earth, and by the shedding of His precious blood solved our sin problem. But even after God has delivered us from sin, His work is not completed. The forgiveness of our sins alone could not fully answer His purpose. Though our sins may be forgiven, we still have not yet returned to God's desire. For this reason, we should not be satisfied and content with just the forgiveness of our sins.

Sin can be likened to the product of a factory, whereas the sinner is like the factory itself. The sin product may be totally destroyed, but as long as the sin factory is still intact, it can easily produce sin again. Our hearts are so desperately wicked that no one is able to expose it to others. This wicked heart of man cannot be cleansed by the blood. It needs to be changed. The efficacy of the blood of the Lord is not in cleansing man's heart but only in cleansing him of all his sins. Blood is not able to clean the unclean heart; it can only cleanse the conscience of the heart, that is, the various guilts in the heart.

When we are saved, we accept the efficacy of the Lord's blood in the forgiveness of our sins. His blood, however, does not change our heart. Hence, if the heart was dishonest before salvation, it will continue to lie after salvation. Should we be greedy before salvation, we will still show ourselves to be greedy after salvation. Unrighteous acts displayed before will mean the same afterwards. If unclean formerly we will be so later. If we were "picky" before salvation, we will continue to be narrow-minded afterwards. After we are saved we tend to think that hereafter our Christian life will be smooth sailing. But it is not so. We soon discover that even though our sins have been cleansed by the precious blood of our Lord, we continue sinning. Therefore, besides using the blood of Christ to cleanse us from our sins God must further provide the means to get rid of the sin-producing factory. It is futile just to deal with sins and not get rid of the sin factory as well. In order to solve the problem of the product (sins), we must deal with the factory (the person himself). Sin has been dealt with, but the man who produces the sins yet remains; therefore, this sin-producing man must be dealt with.

In Chuanzhou a believer, saved just two or three weeks earlier, found himself quite victorious and peaceful. But a few weeks later he was greatly disturbed, for he again lost his temper as before. I spoke to him by way of a parable by saying: Once I met a child whose clay doll got dirty. This small boy asked me to wash it for him. I told him that this was impossible. I could not wash that clay doll of his. But he would not listen; instead, he insisted again that I wash it. So, I could do nothing but wash the doll. The more I washed, the dirtier the doll became. It lost all its hairs. As a result, the child began to wail. I comforted him by telling him that I had forewarned him that his clay doll could not be washed, but that he need not cry because I would buy him a new one. Do we see that we all are like clay dolls? If we are merely washed outwardly we will be even dirtier. In order to solve this entire problem of sin we must commence dealing with the inside.

God's Two-fold Salvation — Blood and Cross

Sin is both outside and inside of man. What man commits is sin; what he hides within is also sin. Man's corruption starts from within. We are like a debtor who owed so much that he was unable to repay. The Lord came and paid off all! Thank the Lord, He paid all for us. This help is truly great. Unfortunately, however, we continue to incur debt. We are debt-addicted. We live by borrowing. Our sins were forgiven, but we continue sinning. For we are born sinners, made up of sin. For this reason, we must not deal with sin only; we must deal even more with the sinner. The blood of Christ deals with sin, and the cross of Christ deals with the sinner.

Blood is for the cleansing of sin: it solves man's outward acts of sin. Without the blood man cannot be redeemed before God. The cross is for putting to death the old man; it deals with the sin nature in man. The Bible never says that blood can wash clean the "I," the "self," the "old man," the "self-life," or the "flesh." For we are like clay dolls which cannot be washed clean. The Bible's way of solving the problem of the sinner is what happened at Calvary: "Away with him!" (John 19.15). This is what the cross means. For the cross puts away the old man, crucifies the old man (Rom. 6.6). Nowhere in the Bible are we told that the blood could wash our own self, that is, the old man with his passions and lusts. Once a friend wrote a poem which declared that "the precious blood washes away lusts and sins." This is incorrect. For passions and lusts need to be crucified (see Gal. 5.24). This is because lust is not an outward act; it is part of the inward nature of man. We need to be careful in distinguishing the different works of the blood and the cross of Christ.

The Bible's Teaching on the Blood

(1) The Old Testament

We will search the Scriptures to find out what it says about the blood. Let us look first at Leviticus 17.11, which says: "the life of the flesh is in the blood; and I have given it to you upon the altar to make atonement for your souls: for it is the blood that maketh atonement by reason of the life." In the Old Testament there are more than three hundred times when blood is mentioned, yet nowhere is the function of the blood mentioned except in this verse in Leviticus 17.11. Here is the only place where is told that the function of the blood is for atonement.

(2) The Four Gospels

Next, we will see how the Gospels speak of the blood. In Matthew 26.28, before His betrayal, our Lord told the disciples: "this is my blood of the covenant, which is poured out for many unto remission of sins." This also speaks about the use of the blood. The blood is for the remission of sins. There, on the night before His death, the Lord explained that the function of the blood is for remission of sins. How different this is from what the Modernists suggest — that the blood is simply an expression of sacrifice. No, the blood of Christ is for remission of sins.

(3) The Apostle Paul

We shall see further how the saints during the apostolic age looked at the blood. First, let us see what the apostle Paul said. In Romans 3.25: "Whom [i.e. Christ] God set forth to be a propitiation, through faith, in his blood, to show his righteousness because of the passing over of the sins done aforetime, in the forbearance of God." The word "propitiation" is "mercy-seat" in the Greek original. The cover of the ark is called the mercy-seat. Within the ark is the law which may accuse us and which condemns our sins; but there is a cover above the ark which indicates that all sins are covered by the mercy-seat, thereby unseen by God. The apostle Paul showed us that the mercy-seat is Christ and that it is set forth in the blood.

Once a Seventh-Day Adventist hanged up the Ten Commandments with the fourth commandment cut off. He used this to warn people that if they did not keep the Sabbath today they violated the fourth commandment. Actually, even should one keep the Sabbath, he shall nonetheless violate the Ten Commandments as a whole if he fails to keep any one of the commandments.

Thanks be to God, for the Lord Jesus is today our mercy-seat. He sits above the law, so that the law cannot accuse us anymore. Had you the ability to remove the Lord Jesus, then the law would again accuse us (see Rom. 8.33-34).

In Ephesians 1.7; 2.13; and Hebrews 9.12-14, 23, all these verses tell us that the blood of Christ is for atonement. Blood is for the washing away of sins. Blood is not for the cleansing of the heart. The human heart is so wicked that it cannot be washed clean by the blood. "The heart is deceitful above all things" (Jer. 17.9a). "All these evil things proceed from within" (Mark 7.23a). So, blood cannot transform an evil heart into a good heart. It is only for the cleansing of sins. Nowhere in the Bible are we told that the blood of the Lord cleanses our heart. But some may respond by saying: "Does not Hebrews 10.22 say, 'Having our hearts sprinkled from an evil conscience'?" But this verse speaks of conscience. For conscience is related to sin. When one sins, his conscience becomes restless. As soon as he sins, he dare not approach God, for there is a breach between him and God. He dare not see God. He is afraid of Him. But the blood of Jesus has already been shed. God cannot be unrighteous in refusing to wash away our sins. We are in debt of sins, and the blood repays our debt. The Lord Jesus has already shed His blood; therefore, God cannot but reckon the debt as paid. He will never ask us to pay again. An "IOU" slip can only demand our full payment; it cannot be used twice. We have this faith and therefore our conscience is at rest.

Someone asked me, "Are we saved by the righteousness of God or by the grace of God?" My answer to him was: We are saved by the righteousness of God. From the birth to the death on the cross of the Son of God — that is a matter of grace. But once the Son was lifted up on the cross, all became a matter of righteousness. The Lord has died; thus, God cannot fail to forgive. If God had withheld His Son from coming to die, He would only have been ungracious. But God has caused His Son to die; so He is bound to forgive us; else He would be unrighteous. Unrighteousness is sin, and God is without sin; therefore, God is not able to be unrighteous. Since the Lord Jesus has shed His blood, God cannot fail to forgive all who believe in the Lord Jesus.

(4) The Apostle Peter

In 1 Peter 1.18-19 the apostle Peter declared: "ye were redeemed, not with corruptible things, with silver or gold, from your vain manner of life handed down from your fathers; but with precious blood, as of a lamb without blemish and without spot, even the blood of Christ." Not once does the Bible tell us that sins are being dealt with by the cross, for it is the old man that the cross deals with. According to the Scriptures, the matter of sins is solved by the precious blood of Christ.

(5) The Apostle John

In 1 John 1.7-9 the apostle John wrote: "if we walk in the light, as he is in the light, we have fellowship one with another, and the blood of Jesus his Son cleanseth us from all sin. If we say that we have no sin, we deceive ourselves, and the truth is not in us. If we confess our sins, he is faithful and righteous to forgive us our sins, and to cleanse us from all unrighteousness." The blood of God's Son Jesus Christ cleanses us from all sins. Our heart is so wicked that even God cannot wash it clean. Yet He does have a way to cleanse us of our sins.

When I was having a meeting in Shantou, one morning early at six o'clock a middle-aged sister came weeping. She insisted on seeing me. She was a widow who had some money but had lived wantonly. She told me the following: "I have committed many sins. My conscience bothers me. I wonder if God would forgive me." I quoted 1 John 1.7-9 to her. I told her that all sins could be forgiven: sins which she considered forgivable or sins unforgivable, sins smooth or rough, sins moral or immoral. Whatever sins she could point out were included in the "all sin" of 1 John. Even the sins she was not able to identify — these were included also.

But she continued by saying: "I am too rotten, I believe that God cannot forgive." So I answered with severity: "Do you realize that you are now doubting God's word? You question the faithfulness of God, you doubt Him who loves you, you are suspicious of the God who cannot lie. Do you see how serious a sin you have just committed? All the sins which you have heretofore committed cannot be compared with this sin you have just now committed. For doubting God and His word is the greatest sin man can ever commit." Immediately she broke out in laughter, declaring: "Then God must have really forgiven us!" Seeing her joyful manner, I for the first time understood the saying: "Laughing breaks out through tears."

The next morning she came again. She said, "My sins are forgiven, but they have many ugly scars. What can I do?" I said to her: "You must read the last part of 1 John 1.9 which says, 'cleanse us from all unrighteousness.' The blood of God's Son Jesus Christ is able to wash away your sins so perfectly that it appears as though you have never sinned. Since *God* will not remember your sins anymore, why should *you* remember them? You should forget your sins, forget the sins of your brothers and sisters, and forget the sins of other people; otherwise, your memory is better than God's."

Towards the end of Revelation 1.5 John wrote this: "Unto him that loveth us, and loosed us from our sins by his blood." God uses Christ's blood to cleanse us from our sins that we might be loosed from them all. Both from the Old and New Testaments we are able to see that blood is there to deal with sin, and is for atonement. The precious blood of Christ has been shed for us. God is righteous. He must forgive all who come to Him with the blood of His Son. Whoever does not believe those words in the Holy Scriptures makes God a liar (see 1 John 5.9-10). He who makes God a liar commits the number one sin. We must not doubt His word. If God has said that our sins are forgiven and our conscience is cleansed, then let us draw near to Him with a true heart in fullness of faith. [*]

---

[*] Note: Message given at Fuzhou, Dec. 15, 1936.

THE CROSS OF CHRIST

Man after the Fall incurs the double problem of sin and sinner. In the salvation of God man's sins are solved by the precious blood of the Lord; but as to the sinner, he has sinned so greatly that God must devise a way of getting rid of the old man. The old nature is hard to change; even God has no way of changing it. It is corrupted inside out. As the leopard is unable to change its spots, so the old man is impossible to be changed (see Jer. 13.23). So far as the salvation of God is concerned: first, sins must be gotten rid of; second, the old man must be dealt with; and third, the new man must be given — that is, Christ the Son of God must live in man. As the Son of God lives in man, sin is easily overcome, because it is as if He himself comes to live again.

The Old Man Is Beyond Cure

"The heart is deceitful above all things, and it is exceedingly corrupt: who can know it?" (Jer. 17.9) Twelve years ago I was having meetings in Xiamen. One day I had a dry throat, so my friend and I went out to buy pears. Each of us bought two pears. We found out that all four pears had worms inside. I tested that friend by asking, "Do you know if these worms entered these pears from outside in or did they come from inside out?" He answered, "These worms must have come in from outside." But I said, "No, these worms came out from inside. Because when the pear tree blossomed, eggs of worms were laid on the flowers. So at the time of fruit-bearing, these worm eggs were wrapped in the seeds. As the pears grew, these eggs were hatched." Is not this the same way in which man's sin comes forth from the heart, as said by the Lord? The number of grievous sins that our Lord mentioned in the Gospel proceed from within the heart (see Mark 7.21-23). The relation between sin and sinner is like the relation between tuberculin and tuberculosis. The blood of Christ washing away our sins can be likened to cleansing away mucus, while His dealing with the old man can be compared to dealing with the lungs. In order to cure tuberculosis the affected lung needs to be removed. So, to cure so corrupt a man, the old man must be removed.

The Salvation of God

"He that hath died is justified from sin"; so says Romans 6.7. Just as we enter into the world by birth, so we can be freed from sin through death. We are born into Adam, therefore we can come out of Adam through death. The cross means riddance. God uses the cross to rid us of our old man. To die with Christ is the only way God uses to put away our old man. The cross alone has the power of getting rid of the old man.

Let us now look at several verses in the Bible that speak especially of the relationship between the cross and ourselves. "Knowing this, that our old man was crucified with him, that the body of sin might be done away, that so we should no longer be in bondage to sin" (Rom. 6.6). This is done once and for all. The word "destroyed" used in the King James Version is too drastic. For in the Greek original, this word means to lay aside or to cut off. It means to cut off employment. So, the most accurate translation should be "to disemploy"; for as our old man was crucified with Christ, the body of sin can become unemployed.

The relationship of sin, the old man, and the body is such that sin is like the master, the old man the steward, and the body of sin the slave. Sin lies inside, the body appears outside, and the old man stands in between. Sin tempts, suggests and seduces; the old man in the middle immediately agrees; and the outside body rushes to carry it out. In this manner, these three operate together. In the deliverance from sin different ways are engaged in for dealing with them. The way of the world is to carefully guard the body from committing sins. This way is dealing with the outside body. There are also the Holiness Church people who advocate the eradication of sin. They presume that they could root out sin so thoroughly that man could never sin again. But the Scriptures make clear that God's way is to deal with the in-between old man by putting him to death. Thus, when sin comes to tempt, suggest and seduce, it lacks the direct power to cause the body to sin. Such, therefore, is God's way of dealing with sin.

Every time sin tempts from inside, it needs the consent of the old man to induce the body of sin to commit a sinful act. God saved us by putting the old man to death, thus causing the body of sin to become disemployed. Further, He plants His own life (as symbolized by the tree of life) within us to replace man's old life so as to enable us to do His will. Thus, when sin again tries to tempt us, we will not be enticed; for the life of Christ lives in us and His life cannot sin. Temptation is ever present, but sin has no power if it is deprived of the assistance of the brain, eyes, mouth and hands. The disemployment of sin occurs through the crucifixion of the old man. Since the old man has been crucified, sin cannot cause the body to sin through the assistance of the old man anymore. So, what God did was to crucify the old man in order that we should not any longer be in bondage to sin. To reiterate: the blood causes us to be saved before *God*, giving us a clean conscience and eternal life. This is what is objective in God's salvation. The cross causes us to be saved before *men*, for it deals with our heart in relation to our practical living on earth. And this is what is subjective in His salvation.

"I have been crucified with Christ; and it is no longer I that live, but Christ liveth in me" (Gal. 2.20a). The cross deals with the "I." "And they that are of Christ Jesus have crucified the flesh with the passions and the lusts thereof" (Gal. 5.24). This verse does not say that *sin* has been crucified, for God uses the cross to deal with the man and all that belongs to him. Man's way is to try to do better through self-cultivation or self-control. God, however, hands over the old man to the cross.

Once I visited a family and saw a child wearing broken shoes. The child wanted them to be repaired. But his mother said, "These shoes are so damaged that they are beyond repair. Go and buy a new pair." Such, then, is the way God deals with the old man.

A full gospel, therefore, is, firstly, the Lord has already washed sins away. "Come now, and let us reason together, saith Jehovah: though your sins be as scarlet, they shall be as white as snow; though they be red like crimson, they shall be as wool" (Is. 1.18). All our sins have been washed away by the precious blood of the Lord. Secondly, we have no means to save the old man, but God has already crucified him. Thus, we ourselves have made our exit through the cross. "Far be it from me to glory, save in the cross of our Lord Jesus Christ, through which the world hath been crucified unto me, and I unto the world" (Gal. 6.14). So far as I can recall, these four verses — Romans 6.6; Galatians 2.20, 5.24 and 6.14 — are the only ones that speak of the relationship between the cross and ourselves.

In Christ

Some may ask that since Christ was crucified two thousand years ago, how can I be crucified together with Him today? First and foremost, we should realize one thing, and that is, God never asks us to look at our crucifixion in our own selves. In the two hundred and sixty chapters of the New Testament, nowhere has it mentioned that we should view our co-crucifixion with Christ in our old man. Even with respect to the blood that washes away our sins, it has nothing to do with us, for we have done nothing. The Lord shed His blood to cleanse us. Someone said, "You should take your sins to the blood and wash them clean." Thank God, it is not we ourselves who today wash our sins, but rather, it is God who has washed away our sins two thousand years ago.

Once in a meeting, someone suggested to sing a hymn entitled, "I laid my sins upon Jesus." Missionaries from various countries were ready to sing this hymn, but I said that I would not sing it because I could not lay my sins upon Jesus. Later on, an elderly missionary mentioned that according to Isaiah 53 it was Jehovah who had laid on Him the iniquity of us all (v.6b); it was not we who laid our sins on Him. So, during that evening meeting this particular hymn was not sung. I hope this hymn would never be sung. We ought to see that our sins are washed by the precious blood of the Lord, and that we have done nothing in the washing.

To illustrate it further, suppose today a friend prays: "O Lord, please shed Your blood for us, please wash away my sins." God cannot answer such a prayer. Such kind of prayer will not save you. For you cannot pray without faith; you cannot ask for things already done. Likewise, if you pray, "O God, please crucify us,"

God will definitely not answer your prayer. You ought to know that God did not crucify you in your own self; rather, He has crucified you with Christ and in Christ. Today we live by Christ. We are saved in Christ, we receive forgiveness in Christ, and we are also crucified in Christ.

Adam is the first man, and Christ is the second man (see 1 Cor. 15.47). There is only one man in heaven as well as there is only one man in hell. In heaven there is only Christ, while in hell there is only Adam. All who are in Christ are in heaven, all who are in Adam are in hell. In the whole world there are only two men. Adam is the first man, and Christ is the second man as well as the last Adam. Formerly we were in Adam, but now we have been placed in Christ. When I spoke in Kaifeng, there was a man there who could not understand the meaning of being in Christ. So I used a parable in answering him: "We Chinese believe we are the descendants of Huang-ti. If during the battle between Huang-ti and Si-iu it was not Huang-ti who killed Si-iu but rather it was Si-iu who shot Huang-ti to death with his arrows, then I ask you this: Where would you be now?" "I would not be here," he replied. True, today you are dead in Adam and are placed in Christ by God.

When I was in Chuanzhou, several brothers asked me: How could we have been crucified in Christ? Christ is Christ, and we are we. There need to be two crosses. So I said to them: Suppose a pregnant woman boarded a bus. She needed to purchase but one ticket; for although there was a child in her womb, the child was still inside the woman. Hence, when the woman purchased the ticket, it was the same as though the child were also buying the ticket. Likewise, because we are in Christ, whatever is done in Him is done in us as well. We have no need to be crucified again.

Someone may ask: According to our experience, why is it we sometimes feel like being in Christ and sometimes not in Christ? Again, I would use a parable to illustrate. There once was a child who was about ten years old. His mother once visited Xiamen ten years ago. I asked the child, "Have you been to Xiamen?" He said, "No." I asked further, "Truly, you have never been there?" He changed his answer and said, "Yes, I had been to Xiamen when I was in my mother's womb. I have never in my own person visited, but in my mother's womb I did visit there." Do you now understand?

Reckon Yourselves Dead to Sin in Christ

"Reckon ye also yourselves to be dead unto sin, but alive unto God in Christ Jesus" (Rom. 6.11). This verse does not say in ourselves, it only says in Christ that we are dead to sin and alive to God. If we look back into *ourselves*, our old man has not died. So, let us say to the Lord, "O Lord, I thank You that in You I am dead." "In whom [i.e., in Christ] ye were also circumcised with a circumcision not made with hands, in the putting off of the body of the flesh, in the circumcision of Christ" (Col. 2.11). This verse says that it is in Christ that we received the circumcision of Christ. How did we receive circumcision in Christ? Just as our sins were forgiven through faith and not by sight or feeling, so also, by faith we received circumcision and were reckoned to be dead. Hence, this matter of faith is explained in Colossians 2.12b: "through faith in the working of God, who raised him from the dead." Our co-death with Christ comes from faith. Therefore, we can come to the Lord and pray: "O Lord, You say that I died in You, and I believe what you say is true."

By Faith

From the time I was called to serve the Lord and up to the end of 1927, I had preached co-death with Christ for already five years. But I did not really know how to die with the Lord. One day in Shanghai the Lord enlightened me, showing me that I am in Him — so that when He died, I too had died. I saw my death to be just as real as His, for when He died I was in Him. I began to see that I really died with the Lord. I joyfully rushed down the stairs, for I was upstairs at the time. I shouted with rejoicing, "O Lord, I thank You and praise You, for I was crucified with You!" I saw it, I believed it, and I received it. A full salvation could not just wash away our sins and allow our old man to remain. Thank God, full salvation includes my old man being crucified as well as my sins being forgiven.

What is faith? There is only one kind of faith in the Bible, and it is believing that a thing is already "done." I have said much this evening, but all will be of no help to you if you do not have this living faith: "I say unto you, All things whatsoever ye pray and ask for, believe that ye receive (Gr. *received*) them, and ye shall have them" (Mark 11.24). Believing is receiving. Believing that a thing *shall* be, *will* be, or *expect* to be done is not true faith. In the spiritual realm, there are two "receives": one is "receive in faith" and the other is "receive in experience." We must receive in faith first before we can receive in experience.

People have three ways to seek healing: (1) if it be a common small illness, seek self; (2) if it be a greater middle illness, seek a doctor; and (3) if it be an impossible big illness, seek the pastor. In reality, this latter kind of seeking — i.e., of the pastor — has little to do with faith. For such seeking is only *expecting* God to heal, not trusting that God has *already* healed. Such prayer of expectation will not obtain the healing. Only the prayer of faith will produce the experience.[*]

---

[*] Note: Message given at Fuzhou, Dec. 16, 1936.

Chapter 6

THE RESURRECTION OF CHRIST

"Reckon ye also yourselves to be dead unto sin, but alive unto God in Christ Jesus" (Rom. 6.11).

"Blessed be the God and Father of our Lord Jesus Christ, who according to his great mercy begat us again unto a living hope by the resurrection of Jesus Christ from the dead" (1 Peter 1.3).

"Verily, verily, I say unto you, Except a grain of wheat fall into the earth and die, it abideth by itself alone; but if it die, it beareth much fruit ... But this he said, signifying by what manner of death he should die" (John 12.24,33).

"There can be neither Jew nor Greek, there can be neither bond nor free, there can be no male and female; for ye all are one man in Christ Jesus" (Gal. 3.28).

We have seen what it means to be in Christ and how we who believe in Him were crucified with Christ. We do not need to seek for means to die ourselves, for in Christ we died.

We have a brother who was a military man before. He told us that according to army regulation any soldier who deserted through fear would be shot. He once talked about this regulation with a few subordinates. He said that army regulation was stricter than any other law. Many soldiers were so ill-treated and even humiliated by their superiors that they no longer could bear them. But once a soldier died, he was freed from the officer. The latter could only suppress him till death and then no more. It is likewise in Christ. Adam's sinful nature exerts great power in us. It opens the door to Satan to buffet and control us. But once we have died in Christ, we are out from under his suppression.

All that we have thus far said relates to the negative side of solving our problems. Now, though, let us consider what God has done for us positively. God had set up Adam as the head of mankind. But after Adam sinned, all men became sinners by birth because all are in Adam. How, then, would God deliver us from sin? His way of salvation is to set up another new beginning, which is Christ. Christ becomes the head of the new mankind, just as Adam was the head of the old mankind. Today, God puts us in Christ to become His people, just as formerly we belonged to Adam. For no person is independent: he is either in Adam or in Christ. In heaven there is but one man, just as in hell there is but one. The question is, Where are you today? Where do you live? Remember that we take our existence from Adam but have entered into Christ through the death of Christ. The resurrection of Christ becomes the beginning of a "new creation." How strange it is that nowhere in the Bible are we told to believe in Christ's death. The Bible only tells us to believe in His resurrection. Paul said, "If Christ has not been raised, then is our preaching vain, your faith also is vain" (1 Cor. 15.14). For Christ's death is negative; it concludes the past; but His resurrection is positive, because it gives us new life so that we can serve God. At the time when Christ was resurrected, all who are dead in Him will also be raised up to newness of life and become new creatures before God.

New Birth by the Resurrection of Christ

1 Peter 1.3 mentions a wonderful thing, which is, that God "begat us again unto a living hope by the resurrection of Jesus Christ from the dead." Today in Christianity people often talk about new birth. Yet few really know how we are born again. Some say we are born again through the cross. But Peter told us that it is by the resurrection of Jesus Christ that we are born anew. In other words, if Christ were not raised from the dead we could not be born from above, for "even when we were dead through our trespasses, [God] made us alive together with Christ (by grace have ye been saved), and raised us up with him" (Eph. 2.5-6a). New birth is provided so as to obtain the life of Christ, and this life is given at the resurrection of Christ. Christ must first die and then be resurrected. Without death He could not be resurrected nor could He give life to us. Thank the Lord. He had died and was resurrected, therefore He could give new life to us.

Let us explain something of the Lord's death and His resurrection so as to provide us with some idea of the victorious life which we have received in Christ. When the Lord was on earth, He used the parable of the grain of wheat. This is recorded in John 12.24. The Lord said: "Verily, verily, I say unto you, Except a grain of wheat fall into the earth and die, it abideth by itself alone; but if it die, it beareth much fruit." In the same chapter, in verse 33, we read that He pointed out that the death of the grain referred to His own death. A grain of wheat differs from a grain of sand. There is life in the grain of wheat, but in the grain of sand there is no life. Yet were a grain of wheat not to fall into the earth and die, it would remain just a grain even after thousands of years. Therefore, one day the Lord Jesus — that grain of wheat — fell into Bethlehem and died at Calvary. Then, in His resurrection we are born again, receiving His very life. Should Christ not have left heaven and come to earth, there would only have been He himself alone. For the Bible says that Christ is the only begotten Son of God (see John 1.18). The only begotten Son means the only Son. God loves His only begotten Son, but He takes additional pleasure in having *many* sons (see Heb. 2.10). God wants His only begotten Son to become the firstborn Son, so that He might have many other sons.

In the Gospel of John, Christ is presented as the only begotten Son of God, but in the eighth chapter of Romans (v. 29) and the second chapter of Hebrews, Christ is presented as He who has become God's firstborn Son. From the human viewpoint we cannot make the same person both firstborn and only begotten son. For the meaning of firstborn implies that there is another son or other sons after this son. And if a son is an only begotten, it means there will be no other son. How, then, can Christ who is God's only begotten Son also become God's firstborn Son? If the only begotten Son remains forever in heaven, then forevermore there will be the only begotten Son. For Him to become the firstborn of God, He must "fall" into the earth. And so, one day Christ "fell" from heaven to Bethlehem and died afterwards. There are two aspects to Christ's death: the first aspect has to do with His atoning death in bearing our sins; the second relates to the non-atoning death in order to release His life.

God's Life Released through Death

Let us read Luke 12.49 which is the deepest verse in the Gospel of Luke. The Lord is recorded there as declaring: "I came to cast fire upon the earth; and what do I desire, if it is already kindled?" He did not say, "I came to atone for sins"; rather, He said, "I came to cast fire." That this fire was cast *upon* the earth shows that the fire did not come from earth but it came from heaven, even from God. Fire points to the life in the Holy Spirit. To cast fire upon the earth is to release the life of God on the earth. And our Lord continued to say as seen in verse 50, this additional word: "But I have a baptism to be baptized with; and how am I straitened till it be accomplished!" "Straitened" in the original Greek means "tightened" or "bound." What the Lord meant was that He came to release God's life, yet He was still in the flesh. He felt tightened or bound, for there was no way to release the life of God. As long as He was in the flesh, God's life could not be released. This was because the life of God was circumscribed by the flesh. Hence, He felt tightly bound up and unreleased.

The Lord mentioned that He had a baptism to be baptized with. Was He not already baptized according to the record that is noted in the third chapter of Luke (see v.21)? Why, then, did He say that He had a baptism to be baptized with? Let us notice that recorded here in chapter 12 of Luke our Lord did not say that He was yet to be baptized. What He said was that He had a baptism to be baptized with. So, it is clear that the baptism here points to His death on the cross (see Mark 10.38). To Christ, His death was a great release. Were He not to die, the life of God in Him would forever be imprisoned and circumscribed. Once He died, though, God's life was released, and became available to men. This was His desire.

The Bible speaks only of "in *Christ,*" not "in Jesus." For we cannot be in Jesus. Jesus is a man, the only begotten Son of God. We can have no part in Him. No one can be in Jesus. Yet one day this man in the flesh, His individual person, was crucified. Although His flesh was put to death, His life was released. When this man was raised from the dead, He became Christ Jesus in whom we can dwell. In Christ not only do we receive His life but we also have died and are resurrected together with Him. This, then, is what the resurrection of Christ has accomplished for us.

Now let us return to John 12.24. We know that the grain of wheat there speaks of Christ. Christ, the only begotten Son of God, died. That grain of wheat died. Its shell was decayed but the life within was released. After a certain period of time, that one grain became many grains. All these many grains come from that first grain of wheat. What was originally the only grain has today become many grains. How did this happen? It was through the fall of the one grain into the ground. The one man Christ died in the world. His body was rent and His life was released. In resurrection, He came to you and me, and we became the many grains. Our new life came from Christ the first grain of wheat. Our new life was distributed to us by Christ. Because of this, we know what is meant by Christ being the head and we being the members of His body. Today this new life is in us, and this life comes from Christ. Such is the process by which God begets us in Christ.

Originally the Lord was the only begotten Son of God, but after His death and resurrection many grains are produced. He thus became the firstborn Son of God; and we, the many grains, became the many sons of God.

On the day of His resurrection the Lord told Mary, "I ascend unto my Father and your Father, and my God and your God" (John 20.17b). Three days earlier, He could not say this; but on the resurrection day He could utter this word. For prior to His death He did not have such a relationship with us; but after He was raised from the dead, He gave His life to us. We now possess the same life and we become the sons of God. Before we were born anew, in Adam there were numberless differences. Now in Christ, we who believe become alike for we have the same life and same nature.

In Christ the New Man

Baptism looks simple, but it involves a great deal. For in baptism, everything is buried: "For as many of you as were baptized into Christ did put on Christ. There can be neither Jew nor Greek, there can be neither bond nor free, there can be no male and female; for ye all are one man in Christ Jesus" (Gal. 3.27-28). For many years, the Communists have tried to overturn the class system, but they fail. They may break the relationship between father and son, but other relationships yet exist. However, in Christ all class distinctions — including national, gender, social status, and so forth — are all eliminated. In Christ we become one. Please remember that this oneness is closely related to the baptism mentioned in verse 27. When do you enter the water to be buried? It is when you confess that your old man has died. As you see that your old man and all which belonged to that old man were crucified with Christ, you ask to be baptized. So, as you enter into the water, you are still one in Adam; but when you come out of the water, you are new in Christ. As we come out of the burial water, all the distinctions which were in Adam remain under water and are buried. We now have Christ as our life. We have become Christians and, therefore, we can be one.

Neither Jew Nor Gentile

Why did Paul refer in Galatians 3 to the Jew and the Greek (i.e., the Gentile)? Generally speaking, the Jews of old were a proud people. They looked down upon the Gentiles as dogs, and even pigs. Even if you as a Gentile had tried to give alms to their poor, they would have rejected your offer. For in the entire world, they alone are the chosen people. Their racial concept was most stringent. It was impossible to unite the Jews and the Gentiles into one. Yet after they have believed and accepted Christ, and are baptized, the Jew in them could not be raised up because only that part which is in Christ will rise. Baptism tests whether you are in Christ. Are you still under national distinction or still under the distinction of slave and free man? During the time of the Roman Empire, the slaves had no liberty whatsoever. The distinction between the bondman and the master was exceedingly great. Nevertheless, all who are baptized into Christ become one in Him. There exist no longer any national, racial, gender, or class distinctions.

Neither Bond nor Free

In Shanghai I have a brother in Christ who cooks for me. At home I call his name; in the meeting I call him brother. Once at the meeting I called him to sit before me. He said, "Mr. Nee ..." I said, "In Christ there is neither servant nor master. You ought not call me *Mr.* Nee, you should call me brother." Also in Shanghai, there was a sister whose husband was yet to be saved. One winter three years ago they two prayed together. The wife prayed first, and the husband followed in prayer. Then the two became man and woman in the Lord. On the day the husband was to be baptized, I spoke to them saying, that from the day they were married till now, their relationship was husband and wife. But after their baptism that night their relationship in Adam was buried. Henceforth they were united into one in Christ.

Once in Canada I met a particular brother. I asked him if his father was saved. He replied that his father was also a brother and that they were now one in Christ. Also, on one occasion at a church meeting I introduced my uncle by calling him brother. In the family there is always the distinction according to the flesh; but in Christ, in the church, there no longer exists such a relationship of the flesh. For we are all one in Christ. I have often said that in the home you call your children children; in the church, though, they are called brother and sister.

In Kaifeng, Henan Province, many government officials believed in the Lord. When I was invited to speak there, one brother introduced to me the Christian brethren there. As he introduced them he identified them as governmental chief so and so. I stopped him and said that we had come out of Adam and have entered into Christ; so, today, we all are brothers. Two of them were chiefs of their government departments. When they came to Shanghai, they were entertained by the brothers. During the meal one brother was going to refer to the guest as chief so and so, but he looked at me and immediately changed his approach by saying, "I am sorry, for it is to be brother so and so." Hallelujah! Today we all have left Adam through death and are now joined with Christ through resurrection. Now we are in Christ. We are the many sons of God and beloved brethren.

No Male and Female

In Christ there is no distinction between male and female. The Bible speaks about the sons of God. Sisters, who are you now? Because of the life of the Son of God in you, you have become the sons of God. True, you are female according to flesh, but now you have in you the life of God's Son which is a son's life; therefore, you sisters are also sons. Once a brother said that we might call brothers as male brothers and sisters as female brothers. His word is quite accurate. True, it is mentioned in 2 Corinthians 6.18b that "ye shall be to me sons and daughters"; but there, however, it has no reference to our relationship in Christ. Hence, it is not contradictory to Galatians 3.28. In Christ we all are sons of God. There is no distinction between male and female. Such is the glorious fact.

The Correct Attitude of Christians

(1) Reckon Ourselves Dead to Sin

This being the case, what kind of attitude should we take today? Romans 6.11 gives us the best explanation: "reckon ye also yourselves to be dead unto sin, but alive unto God in Christ Jesus." Should the phrase "in Christ Jesus" be missing, there would be no Christian faith. Our being dead and our being alive that we talk about here are all facts *in Christ*. I have read Romans 6.11 numberless times, and have even spoken it many times, but I often forgot this phrase of "in Christ Jesus." The fact is that if we are not in Christ, there is no way for us to reckon ourselves as dead nor could we die. We are dead to sin in Christ, not in ourselves.

We should acknowledge to the Lord: "O Lord, when I look at myself I find I am not dead, for I am still alive to sin. Even today I still like to sin. But I thank You, for You tell me that I have died in Christ. For this I now do not believe in myself, I believe I became dead to sin in Christ. I now believe I am already dead." This is faith. Death comes through faith, not by work. It is not that I try to die when temptation comes. No! We have died in Christ, for God had crucified us in Him. In ourselves we are alive, but in Christ we are dead. This death in Him is not a thing of yesterday, nor even of today. It has already been accomplished, for we were already dead in Christ. This is an accomplished fact.

(2) Reckon Ourselves Alive to God

Romans 6.11 says on the one hand that we reckon ourselves as dead to sin. This is the negative side of what we have in Christ. It continues to say, on the other hand, that we reckon ourselves as alive to God in Christ Jesus. This is the positive side of what we have in Christ. In Christ we died and then were resurrected. Resurrection brings in the fruit of the Holy Spirit; that is, to live out the various merits of the life of God. You cannot produce these merits by yourself. You must live by the life of God; for there you will naturally overcome sins and have the fruit of the Holy Spirit. You have no need to pray much. You will be better to praise more. When temptation comes and Satan reminds you that you are yet living in yourself, for you have not died, then you will tell him that you are no longer in yourself but you are in Christ, and that in Him you are alive to God.

Victory Is in Christ

The overcoming life does not come by "reckoning." Victory comes because we are in Christ. Victory is only in Christ. Let me use the illustration of the electric bulb again. The bulb lights up because it is in touch with electricity. The source of electricity comes from the power house. The electric bulb in itself cannot give light. It only lightens up when it is connected with the power house. Let me use another example. Consider the ways the electric tramcar in Shanghai and the motor car run. Neither the tramcar nor the motor car can run by itself. The tramcar runs as it is in touch with electricity, while the motor car runs through the combustion power of the gasoline. For this reason, the power of the motor car is rather limited, for when gasoline is used up, the car stops. Now our life is not like the motor car with limited gas; rather, it is according to the principle of the tramcar. As we abide in Christ, all the riches of Christ will continuously flow into us, and we will therefore have no concern about shining.

All that matters today is whether you are in Christ. In this meeting room, if there be friends unsaved, let me tell you that the moment you enter into Christ and are related to Christ, all His riches will flow into you. Such is the grace of God, that we may receive all without doing anything.

Death concludes everything, it is negative. It concludes the life in Adam and buries all former things. Resurrection is the starting of a new life; it is positive, for it begins a new life in Christ. Therefore, we both died and are resurrected in Him. All is in Christ.[*]

---

[*] Note: Message given at Kulongyu, Oct. 20, 1936.

HOW TO BE IN CHRIST

"Of him [God] are ye in Christ Jesus" (1 Cor. 1.30a).

"God so loved the world, that he gave his only begotten Son, that whosoever believeth on him should not perish, but have eternal life" (John 3.16).

"Now faith is assurance of things hoped for, a conviction of things not seen" (Heb. 11.1).

"Are ye ignorant that all we who were baptized into Christ Jesus were baptized into his death? ... Even so reckon ye also yourselves to be dead unto sin, but alive unto God in Christ Jesus" (Rom. 6.3, 11).

We are still considering this matter of "in Christ" in the Scriptures. The opposite of "in Christ" is "in Adam." The lives and natures of these two realms are totally different. We need to come out of the realm of Adam and enter into the realm of Christ. This is salvation. We live now in Christ. We have seen how God works. Other religions speak of the work of man, but the salvation of Christ does not rely on man's own work. For God works in Christ and has accomplished all things in Him. By the power of the Holy Spirit, Christians are connected to Christ, thus sharing all that is His. Although we ourselves are bad, nevertheless, because we are joined to Christ, all that is His has flowed to us. We are not required to work for anything. God has put us in Christ and caused Him to be our all. This is the glad tidings. In preaching, we must pay attention to truth; but after the truth is known, the way of practicing the truth should also be told. Suppose you tell me how good a place is Xiamen. At the end of your speaking you need also to tell me how I can go there. So, we are now going to see how we can be in Christ.

Of God We Are in Christ

"Of him [God] are ye in Christ Jesus," says 1 Corinthians 1.30a. When our Lord died on the cross, we were already being put in Christ. This is the work of God. As I have said before, I am five feet eleven and weigh one hundred forty pounds. I am an ordinary man, but I have the strength to place chalk into a bottle and to throw the bottle containing the chalk into the sea. How much more powerful is God the Creator, who is able to place us in Christ. God has already done it; it is revealed in the Bible. We cannot comprehend how God did it; nevertheless, we believe it was done.

Of God we are in Christ Jesus. What else is left for us to do? In the New Testament there is one book which specializes in telling us how we can receive life in Christ. That book is the Gospel according to John. "God so loved the world, that he gave his only begotten Son, that whosoever believeth on him should not perish, but have eternal life" (John 3.16). In the Greek original, there is a small word after "believeth" which should be translated into English as "into." The phrase signifies "a believing into." Frequently people ask why in our preaching we do not advise men to do good but are always asking them to believe. Actually, the Bible does not say "believe" or "not believe"; rather, it says "believe into" or "not believe into" Christ. It does not say, I believe in a certain thing, such as believing a certain matter in the newspaper. No, the Bible states that as a man believes, he is believing into Christ. By believing we become one with Christ, that is, we are in Him. So, to be in Christ, we may say that on the one hand this is God's doing but that on the other hand it is our believing into Christ.

The Definition of Faith

Now let us see what faith is. Faith is an extremely important matter throughout the entire Bible. Our so-called faith, however, is likely not that Biblical faith. There are hundreds of places in God's word where faith is mentioned, yet there is only one place in it where faith is defined. It is found in Hebrews 11.1, which states: "Now faith is assurance of things hoped for, a conviction of things not seen." The word "assurance" is not a correct translation for in the Greek original it is a gerund (verbal noun), not a noun. It should be translated into English as "substantiating." The Authorized Version translates it as "substance," but Darby's Bible translates it as "substantiating."

This matter of "substantiating" can be illustrated as follows. We are physical people. We use our five sense organs to contact this physical world. A person without one or several of these five sense organs is unable to know particular aspects of this material world. For this world is full of all kinds of substances and each substance has its color, shape and shade. For example, it is the eyes of our body which identify and transmit them into us so that we come to know these substances. Color is originally outside of man. It is through the human eyes that outside things with color are transmitted into our beings. Color is what the Scriptures would call a "substance," and our eyes substantiate the colorful thing to us. If you talk to blind people about color, and even though there exist many colors in the world, for them no such thing exists. This is not to say there are no colors in the world, it simply means that a blind person lacks this kind of substantiating ability.

Likewise, faith substantiates the various substances of the spiritual world. Today it is God's will for us to substantiate all things accomplished in Christ so that all these things become substances in us. Such, then, is the function of faith. Faith is a kind of substantiating ability that makes it possible for the substances in the spiritual world to be manifested in us. Suppose you talk to a person who lacks faith; such can be likened to an artist mentioning colors to a blind person: the blind man will reject all that the artist has said. Yet this does not mean there are no pictures — no colors — in the world. It simply means that the blind person lacks the special organ within him by which to substantiate the colorful substance. May this not happen to you with regard to the matter of faith.

So, the problem is not whether there are substances in the spiritual world, but whether there is that substantiating organ within by which these spiritual substances can be manifested in us. Even though a person may be blind he still has ears to hear. Yet if I speak into the ears of the blind man about color, his ability to hear will be of no help. All human organs have their special functions. To substantiate spiritual things, faith is the only channel. If we try to use feeling to substantiate spiritual things, we will be totally wrong.

Why is it that you can substantiate spiritual things by faith? It is because Christ has accomplished all and God has placed all in Christ. In the spiritual world God does not ask you to create color or shape, for He has already accomplished them. He therefore wishes you to use your spiritual eyes, that is, your faith, to substantiate them. What the Bible calls faith has the function of substantiating spiritual things.

In practical experience, you may face a problem. Suppose you tell me: "You say I was dead; but as I look at myself, I am not like one dead. On the contrary, I look more like being alive, for I still commit many sins. So, I am very much alive!" Please know that our physical eyes can only substantiate things of the flesh. Faith alone can substantiate spiritual things. Whatever God says is what it is. That is faith. If we use our physical eyes to look at ourselves or feel after ourselves, we can only substantiate things in Adam. Why can we not substantiate all things in Christ? It is because we use the wrong organ. Instead of using faith, we use our physical eyes and fleshly feeling.

Have Faith in God's Word

Perhaps you will ask, "You say believe, but what am I to believe? How does faith work?" Remember, we are to believe God's word. In believing the word of God, it means that when God said in His word that certain things have already been done for us, we believe that what He said was indeed done. Once a missionary asked me, "What is the difference between God's word and God's work?" At that moment I was shaking hands with him with my glove on. I told him, "God's work is like the hand and His word is like the glove. As you hold on to my glove, you hold on to my hand. Likewise, when you hold on to God's word you hold onto His work." Indeed, it is sufficient to hold onto God's word, for the work of God is in His word. If God's hand is not in the glove, then it is in vain to hold onto the glove. But God's work is in His word. So you simply say to Him: "O

God, You say this thing is done. I now believe it is done." God says first, and then you say. God says that in Christ your sins are forgiven; so you say "My sins are forgiven." God says that in Christ your sins have been judged; so you say, "In Christ my sins were judged." God says that the old man is dead; so you say, "My old man is dead." God says that you now have new life; so you say, "I have new life." All which is in Christ will come to you if you so believe.

John chapter 15 says that the Lord is the vine and Christians are branches. To unbelievers this may be taken as something common, but to us Christians this is an earth-shaking affair. For all the fluid of the vine flows through the branches, causing twigs, leaves and fruit to grow out of these branches. Since Christians are the branches in this Vine which speaks of the Lord, they do not need to struggle for growing leaves and bearing fruit so long as they are in the Vine. However, many Christians do not see themselves as branches, so they pray to be branches. Such prayer is futile. For since you are already branches, you cannot pray to be branches. You need to see yourselves as branches already. If you see this, that is faith.

Believe It Is Done

Once I was seriously ill. I prayed: "Lord, heal me. Physicians have given up on me. Now will You please heal me." Many times I had read the promise of God in the Bible. God spoke to me by means of the Bible, it declaring: "Himself took our infirmities, and bare our diseases" (Matt. 8.17). I first asked Him to bear my diseases; later, He gave me promise; but my sickness was not healed. So I again prayed. God rebuked me, saying that I was wrong. Then He opened my eyes to see that the Lord had already borne my disease. So I believed. I no longer prayed, instead I praised. I praised Him for healing my disease, even though in actuality I was no different and my pains were still with me.

Faith is not believing God will do it, instead, it is believing that He has done it — not believing that God *will* heal, but believing that He *has* healed. Faith is believing that God has done all things in Christ. Today, I believe that in Christ God has done all; I accept what He has done as accomplished fact. This is true faith.

Stand on God's Word

There was another time when I was sick, and again I asked the Lord to heal me. God said to me: "The Holy Spirit who dwells in you will give life to your mortal body" (see Rom. 8.11). So I knew God had already healed me. That night I tried to sleep, but I could not do so because my temperature went so high as though my condition had worsened. Satan challenged me, saying: "You said God has healed you, but your temperature has gone up so high that you are sleepless. You said the disease was healed but your pain has increased. You said God has healed you, but there is no such thing." At first I thought I might be mistaken, but later on I realized that these symptoms were an atmosphere created by Satan. So, I just refused them. I resisted Satan by saying: "God indeed said He had healed me. All these symptoms such as high temperature, pains and sleeplessness are untrustworthy. The word of God alone is true. All these phenomena are false. What God says is truth." After I declared this, I was asleep within a few minutes.

Satan may challenge you, saying: "Look at yourself. You are corrupt." Allow yourself to tell him back: "Indeed, I *am* corrupt in my own self. But I now am in Christ, and in Him all is clean." As you stand on God's side, Satan will immediately be defeated.

In studying the Bible, therefore, pay attention to these two things: in Adam and in Christ. These two are totally different, and to recognize the difference is extremely important to Christian living. You need to pay special attention. When your practical living is contrary to the state of being in Christ, you must stand on the side of God's word. Do not ever depend on your feeling, nor even to look at your own condition. You must stand on the word of God, believe in His word; then God will lead you into the riches of Christ.[*]

---

[*] Note: Message given at Kulongyu, Oct. 21, 1936.

Part Two:
Christ In Us

Chapter 1

THE SEED OF GOD

"He [Christ] spake to them many things in parables, saying, Behold, the sower went forth to sow ... When any one heareth the word of the kingdom, and understandeth it not, then cometh the evil one, and snatcheth away that which hath been sown in his heart. This is he that was sown by the wayside.... Another parable set he before them, saying, The kingdom of heaven is likened unto a man that sowed good seed in his field ... And he answered and said, He that soweth the good seed is the Son of man" (Matt. 13.3, 19, 24, 37).

"Verily, verily, I say unto you, Except a grain of wheat fall into the earth and die, it abideth by itself alone; but if it die, it beareth much fruit. He that loveth his life loseth it; and he that hateth his life in this world shall keep it unto life eternal. If any man serve me, let him follow me; and where I am, there shall also my servant be: if any man serve me, him will the Father honor" (John 12.24-26).

(1) The Lord Jesus — the Word, the Seed

Of the first two parables in Matthew 13, the one concerns the sowing, and the other is about the good seed and the bad seed. Concerning the first parable, the Lord told His disciples that the seed sown is the word of God — the word of the kingdom of heaven. Concerning the second parable, He told them that the one who sowed the good seed is the Son of man and the good seed is the sons of the kingdom. Whereas in the first parable the seed is the word of the kingdom — that is, the word of God; in the second parable the seed is the sons of the kingdom — those who are born of God. So, when our Lord sows, He sows not just the word but also sons. At His coming to earth, He not only sends out His word but He also calls out a people and sows them forth as seed.

The Bible calls the words coming forth from God's mouth as the word of God. It also calls the Son whom God has sent as the Word of God: "In the beginning was the Word, and the Word was with God, and the Word was God" (John 1.1). This Word has already become flesh and tabernacled among us, full of grace and truth. We know this refers to the Lord Jesus. Hence, we realize that the word of God mentioned in the Bible refers sometimes to God's spoken word and sometimes to His Son. For the Son is the Word, the living Word, the word of life. In hearing Him, you hear the word; in seeing Him, you see the word; in touching Him, you touch the word. This is what another Bible passage — 1 John 1.1 — confirms to us.

Our Lord Jesus is the Word of God as well as the Seed of God: "Except a grain of wheat fall into the earth and die, it abideth by itself alone; but if it die, it beareth much fruit" (John 12.24). This points to the Lord Jesus, for He is that grain of wheat out of which comes forth many grains: "Having been begotten again, not of corruptible seed, but of incorruptible, through the word of God, which liveth and abideth" (1 Peter 1.23). So, the Lord Jesus is the Word as well as the Seed.

Let us praise the Lord, that He is not only God's Word but also God's Seed. When God sent His Son to the world, He sowed Him as seed. Our Lord Jesus came not only to preach but to be the Word. He is not just a preacher; He is the Word preached. He is not only the Sower; He himself is also the Seed. What God sows is not a few words; He sows a Person. The Lord Jesus is truly the Seed, the Good Seed.

(2) Sons of the Kingdom of Heaven

If people from afar ask us to go there to preach the gospel, it is good that we go with the zeal of the gospel. But be it known that having people to go there and preach the gospel is not enough, for God wants to sow people as seeds there. Do you understand that He wishes to sow you as seed: You are the seed sown. True, God will work in man's heart by His word. We preach the word and plant His word in human hearts, fully expecting a harvest. Yet if we see God's seed as God's word only and fail to see that the word of God is also man, we are still unqualified for His work. If we are careful only about the word we preach, thinking that if we are not wrong in the fundamental truth and are correct in interpretation of the Scriptures we are well able to sow — then we are totally mistaken. Frequently, God's work suffers because the seed in our hand is merely some objective doctrines without causing us ourselves to be transformed into the sons of the kingdom of heaven. For this reason, here is a serious problem: what kind of person you are. God's seed is not just word, it also is your person. Good seed is not only the word of the kingdom of heaven, the good seed is also a person, a son of the kingdom of heaven. May I ask this: How many among us may be God's seed? How pitiful it is that we are mostly objective, lacking in subjective seed. Whether you yourself are able to be God's word is a pressing question. The Lord does not intend to send out a group of evangelists and Bible teachers; His idea is to use men as seed. He wants to sow His own as seed. What will happen, what will be proven if He sows us? "Whatsoever a man soweth, that shall he also reap" (Gal. 6.7b). Those whom we help are oftentimes like ourselves. To turn this thought around, what we reap proves what we sow.

Do not therefore sigh and say, Who will hear our report! Do not mourn that we are helpless because man's ears are heavy, refusing to listen to the pure word of God. Let us ask ourselves who we are. Good seed is not merely the word of the kingdom of heaven; good seed is also the son of the kingdom of heaven who preaches that word. When God sows us, what will we produce? Are we aware of whether the word we preach is like things in a far country to us or is it something out of our personal experience? Do we merely search out a Bible passage and speak on it or do we quote that passage because we have touched spiritual reality before God? The difference between them is vast. Many words are but an engaging in a discussion; but words spoken out of knowing God is seed: It is not something coming out of our cleverness by our gathering various doctrines and then passing them on to others. On the contrary, it is knowing such things before God and, having seen them, words are selected and used to plant in men's hearts. When we preach God's word, it depends not on human eloquence but on how much of God's word has been organized into our own life. The difference is between whether we preach objective truth or we have already had a subjective experience. What many preach is only objective truth, yes this will not affect the hearers. People will only be helped if you are that very word which you preach. For the word of God is not merely something to be understood by the mind. Should it be the latter, the clever will be privileged but all the foolish cannot even be good Christians.

When God's word comes to us, it will be tested. It can be likened to a potter who draws something on a clay vessel. If that clay vessel with the drawing does not go through fire, the drawing will become blurred at the touch of the hand. But God in His grace works and burns. He uses environment and revelation to burn us unto preservation. He works once, ten times, even tens or hundreds of times until one day that word is a burnt word; it has been burned into your life — until one day, you the person are that word. Through the discipline of the Holy Spirit and the revelation of the Holy Spirit, He burns a teaching into a person till that man becomes that very teaching. If anyone meets that person, you will not say he is a man who is able to speak; instead, you will say he is that word. Not till then will he as a person have become the seed of God. But when such happens, God will have found His way to spread that word. Otherwise, it is merely passing some word from one brain to another brain; with the result that the church will be more superficial, more lifeless, and less spiritual. By way of conclusion, let me say that the problem is whether you are able to be God's seed, whether there is part of your life that can be reckoned as God's seed. Should God sow you, what will grow up afterwards? What a man sows, that he will reap. There is no exception to this principle. How pitiful if our fruits are but causing others to understand some teachings without touching life.

(3) The Way to Fruitfulness

God sows for harvest. Let us now see the principle of God's harvesting.

"Except a grain of wheat fall into the earth and die, it abideth by itself alone; but if it die, it beareth much fruit" (John 12.24). This points to how the Lord Jesus died to give us life. It causes us to see that the way to harvest is through death, through the cross. God's purpose in sowing is for fruit, it is for a grain of wheat to produce many grains. He did not send a prophet or many prophets to make clear His teachings; He sent instead His own Son as a grain of wheat falling into the earth and dying in order to bear many grains. Fruit-bearing is not caused by clear teaching, not by memorizing the Scriptures, but by falling into the earth and dying. It is the work of the cross.

The cross is a fact, not a teaching. Real death produces real fruit. Without death it will mean no fruit. The measure of death produces the same measure of life. The number of times of being stricken determines the amount of life that will be manifested.

The word in verse 24 truly points to the Lord himself. In verse 25, however, the Lord explains to us that what He says is a principle which applies not just to himself but is also to be applied to all. "He that loveth his life loseth it; and he that hateth his life in this world shall keep it unto life eternal." Then He makes this even clearer in verse 26a: "If any man serve me, let him follow me." All who serve the Lord fare the same. Know that this matter of a grain of wheat falling into the earth and dying does not refer to atonement, for in the work of atoning we have no part. This refers only to giving up one's own soul life. So, the principle is: death produces life. This is what Paul said: "So then death worketh in us, but life in you" (2 Cor. 4.12).

For this reason, it is not enough for us just to be grains, it is also necessary to see what is our way of fruit-producing. The way of fruit-bearing is not in preaching or teaching alone; it is also sowing the seed. God has not sent His Son to the world only to teach, He has also sowed His Son as grain into the ground. In similar manner, God will sow us as grain here and there.

A grain of wheat needs to fall into the earth and die before it can bear much fruit. Before that grain is sown, you can see it has an outer shell. This shell protects the seed from harm, but it also prevents the grain from bearing fruit. Without the breaking of the outer shell, the inner life cannot break forth. After this grain of wheat has fallen into the earth, a chemical reaction of earth and water begins to work on the grain. A while later, that layer of crust is rotten and broken, but the life within is released. Our Lord himself is that grain of wheat fallen into the earth and, having died, has produced much fruit. Life out of death has happened to the Lord, and it must also happen to us. So, the principle of bearing fruit lies not in preaching but in dying. Whether you have fallen into the ground and died will be known to all who contact you. Is your shell intact or has it been broken? Alas, the hardness in many is natural hardness, and the softness of many is natural softness. Whether hard or soft, it is the shell that withholds life, thus preventing people from touching life. This outer crust can only be gotten rid of through the working of the cross in your life. How impossible to touch the real person if he is unbroken. You may talk to him for an hour, and yet you sense the distance in between; for he has a hard shell. Yet you will touch life if you meet a person who has been smitten, crushed and broken by God and whose natural, soulical part has been broken. Oh, if there be a falling into the ground and dying, then there will be fruit-bearing! Before God, fruit-bearing comes from death. No death, no fruit. You may have tens of thousands of people follow you, yet you may not bear any fruit whatsoever before God. Indeed, the principle of bearing fruit is an undergoing of death. Without death, the grain remains alone. Without death, it will not bear fruit.

May the Lord have mercy on us, causing us to be not only seeds of God but also seeds having fallen into the ground and died so that He might receive much fruit from us.[*]

---

[*] Note: Date and place of delivery of message is unknown.

Chapter 2

THE FULLNESS OF CHRIST

"Ye are all sons of God, through faith, in Christ Jesus. For as many of you as were baptized into Christ did put on Christ. There can be neither Jew nor Greek, there can be neither bond nor free, there can be no male and female; for ye all are one man in Christ Jesus. And if ye are Christ's, then are ye Abraham's seed, heirs according to promise. But I say that so long as the heir ..." (Gal. 3.26-4.1a).

"Because ye are sons, God sent forth the Spirit of his Son into our hearts, crying, Abba, Father. So that thou art no longer a bondservant, but a son; and if a son, then an heir through God.... Now we, brethren, as Isaac was, are children of promise ... Wherefore, brethren, we are not children of a handmaid, but of the free woman" (4.6,7,28,31).

"For freedom did Christ set us free: stand fast therefore, and be not entangled again in a yoke of bondage" (5.1).

"Abide in me, and I in you" (John 15.4a).

"If we have become united with him in the likeness of his death, we shall be also in the likeness of his resurrection. Knowing this, that our old man was crucified with him, that the body of sin might be done away, that so we should no longer be in bondage to sin" (Rom. 6.5-6).

"Even so reckon ye also yourselves to be dead unto sin, but alive unto God in Christ Jesus" (6.11).

"God, being rich in mercy, for his great love wherewith he loved us, even when we were dead through our trespasses, made us alive together with Christ (by grace have ye been saved), and raised us up with him, and made us to sit with him in the heavenly places, in Christ Jesus" (Eph. 2.4-6).

"I have been crucified with Christ; and it is no longer I

that live, but Christ liveth in me: and that life which I now live in the flesh I live in faith, the faith which is in the Son of God, who loved me, and gave himself up for me" (Gal. 2.20).

"To me to live is Christ" (Phil. 1.21a).

"Of him [God] are ye in Christ Jesus, who was made unto us wisdom from God, and righteousness and sanctification, and redemption" (1 Cor. 1.30).

A prayer: O Lord, we feel deeply ashamed under Your light. This is because we live such a poor life while we are really living in Your fullness. We are still thirsty while we are surrounded with waters. Open our eyes to see that fullness is only in Christ. We may enjoy this fullness not because of our faith but because of God's grace; not by our will but by God's election. Neither is it due to our consecration or our obedience but wholly due to Your good pleasure, Your grace and Your mercy. All of us sow by You and all of us reap by You. O Lord, open my eyes that I may really see the fullness of Christ. In Your name. Amen.

Isaac and the Church

The Epistle to the Galatians shows us that the principle of Christian living is to be an heir as was Isaac. As Isaac entered into glory, so also shall Christians do so. As Isaac was born of promise, so Christians, too, become children through promise. Just as Isaac was an heir, so we Christians are God's heirs as well.

The letter to the Romans speaks of how a sinner receives grace, while the letter to the Galatians tells us that after a sinner has received grace, he should not stop there but should advance by the grace he has received. The subject of Romans is about beginning grace, while that of Galatians has to do with advancing and continuous grace. Believers ought not enter in by the Spirit and then try to be perfected in the flesh (see Gal. 3.3). The issue is not in your doing something or giving anything to God, since grace is a looking steadfastly to the Lord's mercy without your effort to improve yourself. It is not a matter of what I shall do; it is wholly looking to the grace of the Lord. As Isaac was an heir and not a founder, so are Christians to be today.

God's Inheritance Is Christ's Work

According to the New Testament the work of Christ is two-fold: one is "we in Christ" and the other is "Christ in us." One is our being joined to Christ, and the other is Christ being united with us. So far as time is concerned, we are first to be in Christ and then Christ is in us. Hence, in the Gospel of John we find the Lord saying, "Abide in me, and I in you" (John 15.4a). We in Christ points to the fact accomplished by Christ; Christ in us indicates the life of Christ in us. Our being in Christ signifies that we as Christians are touched by all the facts accomplished by Christ; whereas Christ being in us the Christians makes it possible for us to experience Christ as our life. Christians being in Christ means that they gain all that He has accomplished in the past; but Christ being in Christians enables the latter to enjoy today what He is and has. For us to be in Christ is to make all things which He has accomplished our own possessions; Christ in us is to make all that He has accomplished our enjoyment.

The Christian in Christ

Our being Christians in Christ explains how God has already put us in a new position. It is a new beginning. It looks from the past up to today. Christ being in Christians begins from today and runs unto future days. Our being in Christ is accomplished by Christ once and for all, whereas Christ being in us continues on to eternity. "Of him [God] are ye in Christ Jesus" (1 Cor. 1.30a), so declares the Scripture; this means that God causes us not only to come out of the old man, our self, the world and Satan but also enter into Christ.

Romans chapters 1-4 tell us about the sinful behavior of man, while chapters 5-8 speak of the man himself as corrupt. To behave sinfully is due to the corruption of the man. Hence, man must die. If we believe we have become united with Christ in the likeness of His death, then we also believe we have become united with Him in His resurrection and ascension. Now we live in the spirit by the law of the Spirit of life. For only in crucifixion, resurrection and ascension is the old concluded. Yet how are you crucified, raised and ascended? It is not by your trying to die, be raised and ascended; rather, it is God's work. It is God who unites us to Christ: "Of him [God] are ye in Christ Jesus." This is a most precious Bible verse and is great in our eyes.

Suppose you put a bank note in a hymn book. If that hymn book catches fire, that bank note inside is also burnt. On the other hand, if you were to send that hymn book to England, that bank note would also end up being in England. All this would be true because the bank note and the hymn book had been united together. Our co-death, co-resurrection and co-ascension is along the same principle. Our natural life — be it good, gentle and patient or wicked and violent — has died in Christ; it is already concluded. Likewise, we have also been resurrected in Christ and have entered into the new creation. Therefore, we have no need to look at our past self outside of Christ.

In 1927, in a room upstairs at Wen-tur Lane, the Lord showed me the matter of co-death in Christ as an accomplished fact. Up to that time, if any one acknowledged the teaching of co-crucifixion, I too would acknowledge it. If someone would say he knew the logic behind co-crucifixion, I too knew it. If others could preach the teaching of co-crucifixion, I could preach the same. If anyone should say to me that I had no experience of co-crucifixion, I would certainly disagree. Yet I realized that I was wrong inside. Many things still troubled me. Yes, I dealt with them continuously. I could not say that I was already dead. I was not that kind of person. For four months I asked the Lord to show me this co-death with Christ and make me truly dead with Christ. Day after day flashes of insight would come to me. Unfortunately, these flashes were not powerful enough. I diligently searched the Scriptures. Every time I read of the verse saying that our old man was crucified with Him, I would follow this up by claiming, "I am already dead." Yet I just could not believe that it was so. I prayed daily. I even stopped serving so as to concentrate on this matter.

One morning, between eight and ten o'clock, in my prayer I suddenly saw that my death with Christ was my union with Christ. It was like that bank note and the hymn book, for those two items were joined in one. My eyes were immediately opened. I mused, "Only one, not two." How, then, could I say that Christ has died but that I did not die? Has Christ died? Christ did die.

Then how about us? I immediately jumped from my chair, shouting: "Hallelujah, I too have died!" I died in the same manner as Christ died. Christ could not be more dead than I or have died more than I. What God has therefore done in Christ was also done in me. Christ died, and I too died. Christ was resurrected, but so I too was resurrected. Christ ascended, so I too have ascended. I rushed downstairs, met a brother. I got hold of him, saying: "Do you know I am dead?" He was baffled and perplexed. I asked: "Do you know Christ has died?" He replied: "I know." Then I told him, "Christ has died, so I too have died." From that day onward I never overturn what I have seen. Such, then, is our inheritance in Christ. To inherit all, it will not be by struggling nor by working. *In* Christ, we inherit *with* Christ. Some may deliver the word of the cross as a teaching, but to some the cross is a seeing, a revelation. All which is of God is wrought in Christ, not in us. But because we are in Christ, therefore, all these things have been wrought in us, too.

Christ in the Christian

Christ in the Christian is related to the future, not to the past. It is in effect from now to future days. Christ in the Christian is not a dealing with things but is a giving to us the power of life. Believers in Christ are meant to enjoy the work and experiences of Christ, while Christ in believers enables them to enjoy the life of Christ, even Christ himself.

Christ in the believer is destined for Christ to live in and for the believer. This is the inheritance of the believer. Christ in the believer has not as its intention that the believer learn and imitate Christ, taking Him as a model and after five or ten years gradually become like Him. For Paul insisted that it was Christ who was crucified and resurrected, not the believer who was crucified and resurrected. It is not the case of a believer himself living through the power of Christ; rather, it is Christ living in the believer as his life.

The Law of Life

Concerning this matter of God causing Christ to be the believer's life, this fact means that there is not the slightest need for the help of the believer's will, because this is a law. Life has its law, and such law is most spontaneous, not manufactured. The law of the Spirit of life is a spiritual law. If to live by this law the believer's will needs to be forced, using strength and struggling, then such a life is definitely not taking Christ as one's life.

It is not enough only to have life. We must also know the law of life. Since it is a law, it is unchangeable. Circumstance, experience and feeling may all change; only law remains forever the same. The law of gravity works everywhere the same. It will not be changed with different time and space. We need not worry about the working of law for it works naturally. As long as we live according to the law of the Spirit of life, that law will manifest its own strength. The secret of Christian living lies not in using the life of Christ, but in letting that life use us. Whenever we are faced with a problem, we can only say to the Lord, "Lord, I cannot, but Your life in me can." We have no need to exert our strength to believe and to do, for this life will naturally manifest itself. So, this is the inheritance given us by God. God's inheritance is none other than Christ.

Christ Is All

Paul in 1 Corinthians 1.30 does not look upon wisdom, righteousness, sanctification and redemption as things but as a person; for all of them point specifically to a personality, even to Christ. This differentiates Christians from people of the world as well as from people of other religions. Christians have Christ working in them and Christ living for them. People of this world must use their own strength, but Christians only need a little faith. For the Lord himself in us is our holiness, righteousness, humility, patience, and so forth. Christ is everything to Christians.

Many lay emphasis on "believe," but such emphasizing degenerates into work or conduct. Many stress obedience; oftentimes, though, it, too, turns to be work or conduct. These, then, come out of man's conduct, not the working of Christ in man. For this reason, believers ought to see that on the one hand we are in Christ, so all the past experiences of Christ are ours; on the other hand, Christ is in us as our life, to live for us. Let us simply believe. This is represented for us in Isaac, for he simply inherited his inheritance and enjoyed it. We thank God, whether it is "we in Christ" or "Christ in us," all is of God!*

---

* Note: Place of delivery of message is unknown; time, 1940.

Chapter 3

THE LIFE-RELEASING
DEATH OF CHRIST

*"I came to cast fire upon the earth; and what do I desire,
if it is already kindled? But I have a baptism to be baptized
with; and how am I straitened till it be accomplished!"
(Luke 12.49-50)*

*"Verily, verily, I say unto you, Except a grain of wheat fall
into the earth and die, it abideth by itself alone; but if it die,
it beareth much fruit" (John 12.24).*

*"I will pray the Father, and he shall give you another
Comforter, that he may be with you for ever, even the Spirit
of truth: whom the world cannot receive; for it beholdeth
him not, neither knoweth him: ye know him; for he abideth
with you, and shall be in you. I will not leave you desolate: I
come unto you. Yet a little while, and the world beholdeth me
no more; but ye behold me: because I live, ye shall live also.
In that day ye shall know that I am in my Father, and ye in
me, and I in you" (John 14.16-20).*

*"We henceforth know no man after the flesh: even though
we have known Christ after the flesh, yet now we know him
so no more" (2 Cor. 5.16).*

The Three Aspects of Christ's Death

The death of Christ covers three different aspects, and they
are (1) substitution, (2) identification, and (3) life-releasing.
Achieving these three aspects of Christ's death makes the
redemptive work of God complete. Should you look at one
aspect only, you will feel insecure as though God's way of
salvation is undependable and incomplete. All three aspects of
Christ's death are extremely important. First, the blood of the
Lord points to His substitutionary death. For accomplishing this,
He has shed His precious blood for us. Second, the death of the

Lord on the cross shows the identification side of His death. We have no part in the Lord's blood-shedding, but we do participate in His cross because when our Lord went to the cross He took us with Him. We need to take notice of the words spoken in the Bible as well as words unspoken there. The Bible says that we were crucified with Christ, but it never says we have participated in Christ's blood-shedding. And hence, we cannot say we have part in the shedding of Christ's blood, though we have truly been crucified with Christ.

Now in the third aspect of His death, the flesh of the Lord points to the life-releasing side of His death. With regard to this particular aspect, it has no relationship to either God or men. For His flesh was given to men in order to release His own life to them. Flesh points to the Lord's life. It reveals how through death the Lord Jesus has released His own life. It is His flesh, not His corpse. The Lord is originally God, but He came to earth, clothed with a body having human life. In order to release His own life, He must shed His human flesh. Is it not written in Luke 12.49-50 that the Lord said: "I came to cast fire upon the earth; and what do I desire, if it is already kindled? But I have a baptism to be baptized with; and how am I straitened till it be accomplished!" The "fire" here does not have reference to natural fire, for it is a special fire. "Casting fire upon the earth" indicates that this fire is not on earth but signifies fire which comes down from heaven. "Our God is a consuming fire," states Hebrews 12.29. So, the fire here represents the life of God, that is, the life of Christ.

Our Lord hoped that people on earth would have His fire, which is His life. At the time He spoke these words, men had yet to receive His life. Hence, He went on to say: "and what do I desire if it is already kindled?" Closely following upon this statement, He continued by declaring: "But I have a baptism to be baptized with." Had not the Lord been baptized already? In Luke chapter 3 we are told that He received His baptism. It was a thing of the past. He had already been baptized almost three years earlier; why, then, should He say here that He had a baptism to be baptized with as though it were yet to be done? We need to understand that the baptism in view here has reference to the death on the cross. For baptism means death; it is a burial.

Viewing the matter from this angle, therefore, the Lord's baptism mentioned in Luke 12 had yet to occur. It had yet to be fulfilled in His life.

The Life-Releasing Death of Christ

In the beginning the life of God filled the universe. After Christ — the Word — became flesh, that divine life was circumscribed by the flesh of His body; therefore, it could not be released. God's life entered first into the flesh of the Lord Jesus. And the Lord looked forward to the baptism by which He could cast off His body and impart His life to men. Luke 12.49-50 are the most precious verses in the New Testament. For before this baptism of the Lord was accomplished, the twelve apostles who so closely followed the Lord could not receive a tiny bit of His life. This is why this third aspect of the Lord's death is related neither to God nor to men, but is vested in the Lord himself.

We will be clearer on this point if we look at John 12.24. There our Lord is recorded as declaring: "Except a grain of wheat fall into the earth and die, it abideth by itself alone, but if it die, it beareth much fruit." The death of the grain has nothing to do with sin, nor does it have any relationship to identification. The death of a grain is solely a life-releasing death. Within the grain is life, yet the life of the grain is circumscribed by its shell. If you put a grain of wheat on a table, nothing will ever happen. It remains forever a single grain. You must sow it into the earth and let its crust be decayed and broken by the damp surroundings. Then life will break forth. It will send its root downward and bear branches and leaves upward. After two or three months it bears a hundred grains. All these hundred grains have life in them, and the life in each grain comes from the first grain of wheat.

Likewise, by the death of God's only begotten Son, God now has numberless sons. Before the incarnation of Jesus, God's life seemed to be abstract and untouchable. Even after Jesus was born, God's life was confined by the flesh. But after Jesus went to Calvary and was crucified, His life was released. The will of God is to make His only begotten Son the firstborn Son so that He might have many other sons. Now, through the death of the only begotten Son, His life is released and produces many sons. The original grain of wheat has borne a hundred grains. And thus there are now one hundred and one grains. So, the sole original grain has now become the first grain. Before the Lord's resurrection God had only one Son; after His resurrection, He had many sons. Before Christ's resurrection, He was the only begotten Son of God; after His resurrection, Christ became the firstborn Son of God. On the day of His resurrection, the Lord told Mary, "I ascend unto my Father and your Father" (John 20.17b). Formerly, the Father was Christ's Father alone. We could not address God as Father. Hallelujah! Since the crucifixion at Calvary and the resurrection of Christ, God's only begotten Son is now the firstborn Son: "For both he that sanctifieth and they that are sanctified are all of one: for which cause he is not ashamed to call them brethren" (Heb. 2.11).

Another Comforter

Now we are faced with a problem. What is God's way for us to receive His life? Let us read John 14.16-20. "I will pray the Father, and he shall give you another Comforter, that he may be with you for ever, even the Spirit of truth: whom the world cannot receive; for it beholdeth him not, neither knoweth him: ye know him; for he abideth with you, and shall be in you. I will not leave you desolate: I come unto you. Yet a little while, and the world beholdeth me no more; but ye behold me: because I live, ye shall live also. In that day ye shall know that I am in my Father, and ye in me, and I in you."

The word "another" means that there is already one, but now comes a second one. The word "Comforter" in the Greek original is "paracletos." "Cletos" means "help," "para" means "in a parallel relationship or manner." In English the word "parallel" conjures up the picture of parallel lines, such as the pathway of a train that has two parallel rails. "Para" means maintaining an equal distance forever, always being alongside. God gives us the second Comforter who is forever with us and always helping us.

"Another" here means "another of the same kind." Christ as the disciples' Comforter on earth will die, leave them, and thus is not forever with them. But there will be another Comforter who will be with them forever. And this other Comforter is the Holy Spirit, the Spirit of truth. The world could not receive Him because they did not see Him nor know Him. But this other Comforter shall be with us forever. Here in John 14.17 lies the difference between the New Testament and the Old. During the period of the Old Testament the Lord could be *with* men, but His presence was outward, quite different from the New Testament presence. According to the New Testament, however, the Lord is *in* men. He is with men by being in men. This is the glad tidings! Formerly, you and the Lord were two separate entities; now, you and the Lord are one because He is now in you.

The mystic part of this passage of the Bible is seen in the change from the pronoun "he" in verse 17 to the pronoun "I" in verse 18. Why is it so? Do take note that "He is I, and I am He." I do believe in the doctrine of the Trinity. The Lord Jesus himself said that He and the Holy Spirit are one. The Lord Jesus today comes to us in the Holy Spirit. Suppose I say that there will be a man coming in a car to this store to preach, and later on I also say that I will come to this store to preach. Such manner of speech reveals that the man mentioned first is none other than I myself. Hallelujah! The Lord Jesus is now in the Holy Spirit. As the apostle Paul said in 2 Corinthians 5.16, "We henceforth know no man after the flesh: even though we have known Christ after the flesh, yet now we know him so no more." In His incarnation, the Word became flesh. Immediately He was circumscribed by time and space. If He was in London, He could not at the same time be in New York. If He was with His three disciples, He could not be with the other nine disciples simultaneously. If He was with the seventy, He was not able to be alongside the hundred and twenty. If He was with the hundred and twenty, He could not be with the five hundred concurrently.

Were the Lord still living in Jerusalem, Christians would have to save money for three or four years before they could go to Jerusalem to worship Him, such as is the case with the Muslim going to Mecca. But the Lord today is no longer in the flesh. Before His death He was clothed with a body. He had a body which clothed Him as it were. But after His death He had put off the body of flesh and is now clothed with a spiritual body. Today the Lord comes to us in the Holy Spirit; hence, He can live in you and in me. I often think how so very complete is the salvation of God that He could be received by us. The Lord is today in the Spirit, and spirit can be everywhere. So we can receive Him. In Acts 2 we learn that the apostle Peter quoted the words from the last sentence of Joel 2: "Whosoever shall call on the name of Jehovah shall be delivered" (v.32a). The apostle Paul has further explained this: "The word is nigh thee, in thy mouth, and in thy heart" (Rom. 10.8a). Please notice that this is because the word is in the spirit; therefore, He can be everywhere today. According to John 14.18b, Jesus said, "I come unto you." This does not point to His second coming (for in His second coming He will come in visible form); rather, it refers to His coming in the Spirit. Today the Lord has already come to us and dwells in us by the Spirit.

Knowing Christ by the Spirit

Some may lament, "I was born too late. If I could have been born two thousand years ago, I would then have seen Jesus." My response to this is, "Even if Peter offered to change his place with me today, I would not accept his offer. Though I am unworthy, I can boast without arrogance that what I now have surpasses that which Peter knew. This is because Peter knew Christ in the flesh, but today I know the One who lives in me." When I was in Europe, I once sailed in the Mediterranean Sea towards Egypt. A friend of mine invited me to tour the Holy Land. I did not accept his offer. I asked myself that if a person visits Golgotha, the Garden of Gethsemane, Sychar, and so forth, would that increase his knowledge of Christ? No, not a bit. So, I decided against visiting. Paul once said: "We henceforth know no man after the flesh; even though we have known Christ after the flesh, yet now we know him so no more" (2 Cor. 5.16). So, today we do not know Christ in the flesh, knowing Him only outwardly; on the contrary, we know Him in the Spirit.

How clear is the statement given in Romans 8.9b — "if any man hath not the Spirit of Christ, he is none of his." Who are the sons of God? Those who became sons of God through the only begotten Son of God. It is because we are in His Son, and in Him we become many sons. All the children of God in the Bible are described as masculine in gender. Why, then, in 2 Corinthians 6.18 does it say, "[I] will be to you a Father, and ye shall be to me sons and daughters"? This is because this verse has nothing to do with our position in Christ. Hence it reads: "sons and daughters." But in Christ, there is no such gender distinction. We are all sons of God for we all have received the life of the Son of God. Hallelujah! The life of God's Son is in us. This makes all of us God's many sons. The life in the sisters is the same as the life in the brothers.

"As many as received him, to them gave he the right to become children of God, even to them that believe on his name" (John 1.12). This verse points particularly to how we receive God's life; it does not speak about how a sinner receives salvation by accepting Christ as his Savior.

Now we will draw a conclusion from all which has been said. Both the blood and the cross aspects of Christ's death have the "sinner" in view, while the flesh aspect has reference to "man." The blood of our Lord deals with sins. It signifies the substitutionary work of the Lord, which is towards God. It is objective in nature for cleansing, forgiveness and justification. It is passive in the sense that we receive by faith. The cross deals with the old man. It works in men. It is the work of identification of the Lord. It is subjective in nature in the sense that it involves the cutting off of the flesh; but it is also objective in the sense of this work having been wrought in us through our believing. The first two aspects are for getting rid of our obstacles. The flesh aspect of our Lord's death is for dealing with man in that it gives life to him, even life within him. It is the life-releasing work of the Lord. This third aspect of His death is subjective in nature in that it results in releasing, supplying, maintaining and producing. We likewise receive this aspect of Christ's death by faith so as to fulfill the purpose of God. We must learn to thank and praise God more for the fact that His work has already been accomplished.[*]

---

[*] Note: Message given at Fuzhou, Dec. 17, 1936.

Chapter 4

THE VICTORIOUS LIFE

"When Christ, who is our life, shall be manifested, then shall ye also with him be manifested in glory" (Col. 3.4).

"To me to live is Christ" (Phil. 1.21a).

"I have been crucified with Christ; and it is no longer I that live, but Christ liveth in me" (Gal. 2.20a-b).

"Of him [God] are ye in Christ Jesus, who was made unto us wisdom from God, and righteousness, and sanctification, and redemption" (1 Cor. 1.30).

We have seen in the Bible that what God has provided for man is always the best. The blood of Christ speaks of how He served as our substitute and suffered the righteous judgment of God. The cross of Christ crucified us — our old man — together with Him. The flesh of Christ rent on the cross released His life to us. Unfortunately, many consider Christ's life in us merely as the work of strengthening us. They fail to know clearly the salvation of Christ. After they are saved they think of imitating Christ, just like doing a copy book. If they succeed, they become good Christians; if they fail, they are not good Christians. So they ask the Lord to give them strength that they might be Christ-like, with holiness and lowliness, just as their Lord who had such a heavenly life and prayer life.

What people expect is that they themselves can do it. If you were to tell a person that he cannot do it for he is totally undone, he would not like what he has heard. Many have scolded me, Watchman Nee, as bad; but instead of getting angry, I will tell them that their scoldings are inadequate, since I am far worse than their accusations. For in this inch-wide heart of mine I am able to commit all the sins in the world. Therefore, God has already given me up as helpless. Do you see this? For this is what man is. For this reason, God does not want man to live by his own life; instead, God will give him Christ to be his life that he may live out Christ's life. Such, then, is the salvation of God.

What is life? Life is something in you which, when it is removed, you can no longer exist. Christ is my life. Removing Him from me, I cannot live any longer. Paul had not said, "I will be like Christ, I will depend on Christ, I will imitate Christ by His power, I will take Christ as my model." No, but Paul did say, "Christ is ... our life" (Col. 3.4) and "to me to live is Christ" (Phil 1.21a). Paul acknowledged that his life was Christ. He lived because Christ lived in him. Take away Christ and he will live no more.

Victorious Life Is Christ

What God has prepared for everybody in the gospel is causing Christ to be our life. So now, we will inquire, What is meant by Christ our life? "I have been crucified with Christ" (Gal. 2.20a) is not a goal for us to arrive at. For this word can never be attained by us; it is the work of the Lord. Following upon this statement is the next: "It is no longer I that live, but Christ liveth in me" (Gal. 2.20b). In other words, now it is Christ in me living for me. For "the heart is deceitful above all things, and it is exceedingly corrupt" (Jer. 17.9a). Unless Christ lives in you, you cannot help but sin. The human heart is so corrupt that it is beyond repair. So, God must put it aside and replace it with Christ as the life.

What, then, is victorious life? The Son of God in us overcomes sins for us — and this is victorious life. The life that overcomes is not in the Lord having given me power that causes me to be holy and clean. No, victorious life is Christ living out His obedience and gentleness — in me and for me. Do you see the difference between Christ giving you strength to be humble and Christ living in you as your humility? The difference is as vast as that between heaven and earth. Blessed are you if you see it.

When I was having meetings in Yantai, a mother told me: "I am able to be victorious in many things, even able to confess to my mother-in-law and be reconciled. But I cannot overcome the noises made by my two children. I can be patient to their voices for five or six times, but after that I lose my patience. Can you pray for me, asking God to give me a better environment that I may overcome?" My reply was: "I cannot ask God to make you victorious because this God will never do. He will instead cause you to be defeated. For victory comes from God. It is Christ in you as your victory. It is not God helping you to overcome. If victory comes from you, you can bear the voices made by children four times, but at the fifth time you explode. Suppose the Lord comes to your home and takes care of the children for you. Will their voices be unbearable to you? You will be more than conquerer even to the hundredth time."

Victory Is: Christ Lives in Us

Victory is the Lord Jesus living in us. Because He lives in me, He can overcome for me. There will not be any temptation which He cannot conquer. God has not given me Christ to be my model; He gives Him to me as my life. Four years ago I was in New York. There was a physician and his wife. They had four children. The wife was around forty years of age and was most humble. She said to me: "You must pray for me, asking God to grant me patience. My four children have tested me beyond measure. When one child was naughty, I could bear with it, even to the extent of bearing the naughtiness of two children. But when three children got naughty together, anger rose to my head. If four got naughty at the same time, I lost my temper." I asked her, "What do you lack?" She replied, "Without doubt I lack patience." So I continued by asking her, "You have been asking the Lord to give you patience. Has He answered your prayer?" "Not yet," she answered. So, I told her straightforwardly: "The Lord will never hear such a prayer of yours, not only in time past but also in the future. Formerly you were not patient, later on you will still be impatient. What you lack is not patience." "What do you mean?" she inquired. "I do not lack patience? What do I lack, then?" I replied, "What you lack is Christ, not patience, gentleness or quietness." For patience is Christ. True humility, gentleness and holiness are Christ.

When I was in Shanghai, a brother told me, "I am not able to be patient. How can I be patient?" I said to him: "In Shanghai there is a factory manufacturing toothbrushes. They only do wholesale business, no retail. Our God is like that. He only provides wholesale, not retail. If you ask Him for a little patience, He will not give it to you. For He has placed all virtues in Christ. By believing and receiving Christ you have Christ and all these virtues are yours. According to 1 Corinthians 1.30, God gives me Christ to be my sanctification. It is not I who can be holy, but it is Christ in me to be my holiness. He lives out holiness in me and for me. Should someone see this, I will shake hands with him and congratulate him as the most blessed person in the world. But by you still living yourself, attempting to be holy, you will be miserable. With Christ in you, you will have found the secret of victory. Such is the victory God gives to us."

The Nature of the Victorious Life

(1) Exchange Not Change

Let us see the nature of the victorious life. First of all, we shall see that the victorious life is an exchanged life, not a changed life. Victory is not due to my being changed; rather, it is because I have been exchanged. We all want to change, but God shows us that we are beyond repair. God has already given up hope on us. He reckons us as unchangeable. There is a proverbial saying in the Fuzhou dialect which says "Changeless till death." It means that the person is forever unchanged. Thank the Lord. He shows us that it is not our life changed, but He has had our life exchanged.

When I was in Shanghai once, I bought a watch. The store gave me a paper guaranteeing that they would repair without cost any damage to the watch within two years. I bought the watch and brought it home. On the next day, in the morning, I discovered that the watch ran two hours late. I took it to the store and told them this. They said, all right, we will repair it. After two days I got it back. After using it a day, I discovered it was one hour late. So, I took it back again. After it was again repaired, I found out the next day that it stopped running entirely. I took it back again and asked them to notice that the watch had stopped running altogether. They said to me, "All right, say no more, we will repair it." I received it back after a week, but I noticed the next day that it was three hours too fast. So, I went to the store and said to them, "I have had this watch for twenty days now. Of these days it was in your store for fourteen and in my possession for only six. Is this watch yours or is it mine? If you cannot repair it, please exchange one for me." Yet they told me in response: "We have no obligation to exchange; the guarantee is only for repair. If the watch does not work right, you may bring it to us and we will be responsible to repair it for you until the two-year guarantee is over."

Do you now see that repair and exchange are totally different? Repair is to correct the damage, while exchange is to discard the old and provide a new one. Repair is the thought of man; exchange is the salvation of God. Man usually thinks of asking God to give him strength that he may change to be better, not realizing that all people are like that bad watch which was beyond repair. It needed to be exchanged for a new watch. The salvation of God lies not in helping us to change for the better and to assist us to overcome, but to overcome by substituting Christ for each one of us. For God will never do the work of changing us; He will only do the work of exchanging our old life for His life.

Once I was in Yantai, speaking especially to Western people. After I mentioned this matter of overcoming, someone raised the question: "How can a life be changed?" I told them that victory came not by changing life but by exchanging life. People have always thought of changing themselves; in God's view, however, men were so corrupt that they were beyond changing. It was not the case of Adam being changed to become a son of God, nor a tare [weed] being changed to become a stalk of wheat. It is instead the case of Adam being exchanged for a son of God and the weed being exchanged for a stalk of wheat. God has used the cross of Christ to crucify our old man so that Christ in us overcomes for us. Our life is to be totally exchanged, not that it be somewhat changed.

I cannot but mention another story. Last year in Shanghai a foreign missionary came and told me about a missionary friend of his who served in a school. This friend was in Shanghai for almost six years but he could not maintain a good relationship with either his colleagues or his students because he had such a bad temper. Neither the school nor the missionary society knew what to do. Accordingly, the society decided to send him back on November 1. So the missionary who had told me all this wanted me to help his friend. He said to me: "That person is so strange that he never laughs. Every time he meets people, he gives them a bad face. He is angry from dawn to dusk. Everybody grew afraid of him. All would walk away at the sight of him. For almost six years he has acted like this. No one in the school can work with him. All four hundred plus students in the school are afraid of him. Wherever he goes he quarrels with people. I am afraid he is demon-oppressed. Mr. Nee, you know the truth of overcoming. Is there any way you can help?" After I heard, I felt joyful in my heart; for confronted with an impossible person, it was clearly impossible for man to solve but possible for God. God specializes in healing the impossible. So I told the missionary I would see his friend.

After two days I was home alone, and this man was brought to me and was introduced to me. When I first saw him, I was almost frightened to death. I had never seen a person like him in my whole life. I realized that what the missionary told me was true. When I saw him a chill came over my whole body. I was afraid that this was really a case of demon oppression. Yet as he saw me, his tears began to fall incessantly, and he told me: "Nobody wants me." As he cried, his face became so ugly as though he were losing his temper.

I asked him: "How do you feel yourself?" He answered: "I often purchase things for others, I preach the gospel, I pray for the people. When people get sick, I pray for them, and they are healed. But I do acknowledge that my temper has been somewhat bad." "A little bad?" I inquired. "To be honest with you, it is extremely bad! I have a temper of a wild animal," he said. I continued by asking, "Is that so since childhood or does it happen now?" He replied: "If I remember well, I have had a temper since I was four years old. My mother died when I was thirteen, and my temper got worse. Up to this day, I am helpless. This not only dishonors the Lord but I sin continuously, and I feel I am the most pitiful person in the world because no one is willing to nod his head or talk with me." As he spoke, he wept. On the contrary,

I began to laugh. "Don't laugh at my bad temper," he said. "I do not laugh at your bad temper, I laugh with joy. I rejoice because of your helplessness. This opens the way for God to work," I replied.

So I next said, "There is no difficulty with a situation like yours. It is not impossible for you to overcome, if you really want it. It can be done in a minute. The question lies not in how good or bad you are, how able or unable you are, but in whether God is able. For overcoming depends not on you yourself, it wholly depends on the Lord. It is all because Christ in you can overcome for you. It is by Christ, not by you, that you overcome." Then he said, "What do I need to do to control my temper?" I answered him this way: "You must do nothing. Let Christ do all. Let Christ in you do it for you. Look not at your own self. Look to the Christ of God alone. God will make you victorious." We had talked for four and a half hours, but the light failed to penetrate his mind. So we knelt and prayed. He prayed in this way: "O God, I am truly totally corrupt, I give up hope on myself, I am helpless. Henceforth, I will not trust in myself. I cannot overcome. O God, unless You overcome for me, I am forever undone. Hereafter I give myself up. O God, You yourself be responsible!"

After he had sincerely prayed, he asked me again, "What must I do afterwards?" I told him: "Do nothing." Then he smiled. After going a few steps, he turned around and said, "Is it really that I do nothing?" I answered: "True, it is well if you do nothing at all. When Satan comes to tempt *you* to be patient, you must say: 'I cannot be patient. Christ, will You please be patience for me!'" "Yes, yes," he murmured. "I need not do anything. Should I be delivered of my temper, it must be God, not me." A few days later, I asked about his condition. One person told me: "Strange, really strange! The whole school is now enjoying such peacefulness as never before. For the past six years, we have never seen him so tranquil. We have not even heard any sound from him. God has indeed manifested His wonder and power in him." Let me say that if this man can overcome, everybody can overcome.

After a few days he came to our meeting. He, too, could now laugh. Later on, his colleagues and students bore witness of his having totally been exchanged for Christ. Due to his total transformation the missionary society decided not to send him back.

We do not overcome sins by using prayer and Bible study or power. I do not say that we do not need to pray and to read the Bible. Prayer and Bible reading have their own benefits, yet they are not the power of overcoming sin. Matthew chapters 5-7 say that we are sons of God; they do not say that we make ourselves sons of God. For if God demands us to become His sons, this we could never do. "Even so let your light shine before men; that they may see your good works, and glorify your Father who is in heaven" (Matt. 5.16). Your good works bring glory to God: this proves that it is God who works in you, therefore glory must be given to Him, not to you. If another brother gives a good message, will people praise me instead? We have good works, but why do people glorify God instead? The only reason is because all these good works come from God, and they are His doing.

(2) Obtained Not Attained

Another nature of victorious life is that it is obtained, not attained. You can only obtain victory; you cannot attain it. Obtaining is receiving, while attaining requires a long walk. Did you spend time and effort in getting your salvation? No, you simply received and you had it. Likewise, victory is obtained without any effort of reaching after it. The meaning of "obtain" is that as soon as you receive, you have it. "Thanks be to God, who giveth us the victory through our Lord Jesus Christ" (1 Cor. 15.57). Thank God, victory is not attained with effort, victory is given us by God. As God offers it to us, we take it with stretched-out hand.

Charles G. Trumbull was quite spiritual. He acknowledged that the victorious life is truly a miracle. Once he testified to a church elder that since he had accepted the Lord Jesus as life, he had not once lost his temper nor did he have any inclination to do so. That elder replied, "I believe this thing is true in your life, but to me it is not a reality." Mr. Trumbull asked him to pray together with him. Afterwards, that elder himself bore witness, saying: "Never in my life have I experienced anything like what happened that evening. It is truly a miracle! There is no need to struggle, to exert strength, nor even to desire it. This is really marvelous, it is a miracle." Not long afterwards he wrote a letter to Mr. Trumbull saying that in the place where he worked, there was evil influence. Whereas formerly he had had to suppress himself, now, after he had prayed with Mr. Trumbull, he did not need to suppress himself any more, nor did he have any thought of doing so.

Formerly there was an Anglican minister in England. His name was H. W. Webb-Peploe. One day his daughter died. After the burial he became aware that the next day would be the Lord's day. What kind of message should he prepare to deliver to the people? He thought of 2 Corinthians 12.9 and was thinking of using "My grace is sufficient for thee" as his subject. He knelt down and prayed for God's blessing of this subject. While praying, he asked himself: "Is the grace of God really sufficient for me? If it is not true for me, how can I tell people that God's grace is sufficient for them? My daughter is dead. I am troubled. My heart aches. I cannot submit. This shows that God's grace is not sufficient for me. I cannot lie." He was thinking of changing the subject, but he was pressed for time. So he prayed, asking God: "O God, cause me to experience Your sufficient grace, make Your grace sufficient to me." He prayed for a long time, but there seemed to be no effect. Right at that moment, he unintentionally saw a framed Bible text hanging on the wall. This had been given him by his mother. It was exactly that verse in 2 Corinthians 12.9, "My grace is sufficient for thee." The words "My" and "thee" were printed in black color, only the word "is" was in bright green. Suddenly he was enlightened. "Did not God say, 'My grace is sufficient for thee,' and yet I have said, 'Your grace is not sufficient for me.'" He immediately confessed his sin before God: "O God, You say 'My grace is sufficient for thee'; yet I am still praying for Your grace to be sufficient for me." He confessed his sin to God on the one hand, and thanked and praised Him on the other, now declaring that His grace was indeed sufficient for him. He was full of joy and thanks. The next day he stood in the pulpit and preached the best sermon of his life. Some people asked him what was his secret. He replied that after his daughter's funeral, he saw what "believe" meant. "Believe" is not asking God to fulfill His promise; rather, it is praising and thanking Him for He has already said so. Since that incident, his life was completely different.

The entering of God's life enables you to live on earth just as His only begotten Son had lived in Nazareth in His day. God will raise up a class of new creatures that have His Son as life, hence living out the Son's life. "I can do all things in him that strengtheneth me" (Phil. 4.13). The word "strengtheneth" means "empower." So, "I can do all things in him who empowers me." There will be nothing too hard for you because today there is One in you who empowers you, and that One is almighty. Our Lord does not want us to be ordinary or common people. He wants us to have a God-like life that is capable of saying what ordinary people cannot say, do what they cannot do, live in a way beyond human effort, and face situations with which common people are unable to cope. With Christ in us we can live such a life.

Allow me to say something that will offend people. Today, there are too many in the church who seem to be dispensable. They are those whom God cannot use. The reason lies in their not having this victorious life. They can neither testify to the world about the life of Christ nor help others to overcome. May we ask God to give us light, seeing what the nature of victorious life is. Thank God, salvation is full and complete. He has not only saved us from the punishment of sins, He also has delivered us from the bondage of sin. God's way of salvation is letting Christ suffer the judgment of sins for us, crucifying our old man together with Christ, and releasing His life to us that He might live in us. Christ in us is our victorious life.

Thank the Lord, that though His throne is in heaven, He is also in our hearts. Thank the Lord, that though He lives in heaven, He also lives in us. He fulfills in us all the things pleasing to God. All the great and difficult commandments given in the Bible are not meant for men to keep because the Lord himself will keep them for us. The harder the commandment, the better proof of the Lord's sufficiency. Alongside Matthew 22.37 ("Thou shalt love the Lord thy God with all thy heart, and with all thy soul, and with all thy mind"), Margaret E. Barber wrote the following sentence: "O Lord, I thank You for giving this commandment." This is because she knew the Lord would do it. Only Christ can fulfill all the commandments in the Bible. Thank the Lord, Christ is our life. Christ is our victory.[*]

---

[*] Note: Message given at Fuzhou, Dec. 19, 1936.

Chapter 5

HOW TO EXPERIENCE
THE VICTORIOUS LIFE (1)

"A certain ruler asked him, saying, Good Teacher, what shall I do to inherit eternal life? And Jesus said unto him, Why callest thou me good? none is good, save one, even God. Thou knowest the commandments, Do not commit adultery, Do not kill, Do not steal, Do not bear false witness, Honor thy father and mother. And he said, All these things have I observed from my youth up. And when Jesus heard it, he said unto him, One thing thou lackest yet: sell all that thou hast, and distribute unto the poor, and thou shalt have treasure in heaven: and come, follow me. But when he heard these things, he became exceeding sorrowful; for he was very rich. And Jesus seeing him said, How hardly shall they that have riches enter into the kingdom of God! For it is easier for a camel to enter in through a needle's eye, than for a rich man to enter into the kingdom of God. And they that heard it said, Then who can be saved? But he said, The things which are impossible with men are possible with God" (Luke 18.18-27).

"He [Jesus] entered and was passing through Jericho. And behold, a man called by name Zacchaeus; and he was a chief publican, and he was rich. And he sought to see Jesus who he was; and could not for the crowd, because he was little of stature. And he ran on before, and climbed up into a sycomore tree to see him: for he was to pass that way. And when Jesus came to the place, he looked up, and said unto him, Zacchaeus, make haste, and come down; for to-day I must abide at thy house. And he made haste, and came down, and received him joyfully. And when they saw it, they all murmured, saying, He is gone in to lodge with a man that is a sinner. And Zacchaeus stood, and said unto the Lord, Behold, Lord, the half of my goods I give to the poor, and if I have wrongfully exacted aught of any man, I restore fourfold. And Jesus said unto him, To-day is salvation come to this house, forasmuch as he also is a son of Abraham.

For the Son of man came to seek and to save that which was lost" (Luke 19.1-10).

We have seen what victorious life is. Victorious life is Christ, it is Christ living in us. To overcome is not due to our being helped to be like Christ; rather, it is Christ living in us and overcoming for us. Victory comes not because we have received power to be humble and worry-free; it comes through Christ in us becoming our humility and peace.

Why is it that many Christians today fail to obtain these provisions of God? In fact, each and every one who believes is already in the good of what the blood, the cross and the flesh of Christ have accomplished for us. Yet, in experience, many still fall short of their full inheritance. It is like a person who has purchased two packages of things, but he opens only one of them and leaves the other unopened till perhaps after three or five years. How very pitiful that many Christians act the same way towards God's wonderful provisions. Now we want to use these two passages of Scripture to explain how we can experience this victorious life.

Impossible with Man but Possible with God

It is said in Luke 18.26: "Then who can be saved?"; but in Luke 19.9 we read: "To-day is salvation come to this house." In chapter 18 is shown a rich young man who was also a ruler. He inquired of the Lord as what he must do in order to inherit eternal life. The Lord answered him by suggesting that he must keep the commandments — such as no adultery, no killing, no stealing, no false witnessing, but honoring the parents. When the young man said that he had observed all these commandments from his youth up, the Lord answered by saying: "One thing thou lackest yet: sell all that thou hast, and distribute unto the poor...." This young man left exceedingly sorrowful after he heard this word. Consequently, the Lord made a comment: "How hardly shall they that have riches enter into the kingdom of God! For it is easier for a camel to enter in through a needle's eye, than for a rich man to enter into the kingdom of God." The disciples hearing this moaned, "Then who can be saved?" "The things which are impossible with men are possible with God," answered the Lord.

The rich man in Chapter 19 differs from the rich man in chapter 18 in that the former was a tax collector while the latter was a young heir. According to general estimation the older man in chapter 19 should be more miserly than the younger man in chapter 18; this was because the latter had less life experience in knowing the value of wealth. Yet what Zacchaeus in chapter 19 did was that which the young ruler in chapter 18 failed to do. Why was it so? According to common knowledge, a young man usually is more liberal in spending and is not a great lover of money. But this young man was different, for he held on tightly to his money. Indeed, not just the young ruler could not give up his money, the older man Zacchaeus was no different, for he, too, was not able to let go of his wealth. Nevertheless, in Zacchaeus's life there was the work of the Lord, as it was said in 19.9: "To-day is salvation come to this house." This indicates that Zacchaeus was able to overcome the grip of wealth on himself due to the work of God. It was because the salvation of God had come to him. Immediately thereafter, the Lord said: "he also is a son of Abraham." The phrase "son of Abraham" signifies a man with faith. So what Zaccheaus did was done by faith, not by his own work.

Realizing — Impossible with Men

The Lord Jesus asked the young man to sell all that he had and give to the poor, but he could not do it. The Lord Jesus had not asked the older Zacchaeus to give away his wealth, yet this older man gave much of his money away quickly. What made such a difference? The difference lies in the words, "The things which are impossible with men are possible with God." That young ruler is a most excellent example of the "impossible with men" concept found in the first part of Luke 18.27, while Zacchaeus is an excellent case of the "possible with God" concept found in the second part of that same verse. So, the first secret of victory is the acknowledgment which is contained in the phrase, "impossible with men." We need to learn to recognize that it is indeed impossible with men.

The Lord's purpose was not in asking this young man to actually sell all as a condition to inherit eternal life; instead, He wishes the young man to realize that such an act is impossible with men. That young man was quite good. He considered himself extraordinary because he had kept the commandments. The Lord intentionally placed before him something he lacked. Many who are saved are able to overcome many of their old sins, except a few. Why could they not overcome their few old sins? The Lord allows this to happen in order to teach us the lesson of realizing that such overcoming is impossible with men. It can be likened to running a race of high hurdles. You can jump over every hurdle except one or two. *God* knows you cannot, but *you* do not realize your inability. You may be able to keep the Ten Commandments, but the Lord places before you the eleventh commandment which you are unable to keep.

With respect to us all, there seems to be one or two sins that we cannot overcome. Such sin or sins become our special problem. Once in Shanghai I went out to purchase something in a store. As I left my house I met a brother and I nodded my head to him. On the next street I met him again. So, I nodded to him again. At the front of the store I again met him and nodded. When I left the store, once again I met him and nodded to him. As a matter of fact, I nodded to that brother ten times within an hour. Our sinning occurs exactly in the same way. We seem to encounter the same sin frequently. We sin the same sin today and tomorrow and the day after tomorrow. We are so familiar with the same sin. Our sins seem to be special, not general. A hard person is always hard. A woeful man is always woeful. A proud man is always proud. A worrying man always worries. A despiteful man always despises. A man with a quick temper is always quick to lose it. Each person lacks at least one thing. And God wants us to see that it is impossible with men.

Once when I was in Yantai there was a medical doctor's wife there who was seeking for a victorious life. During a whole month she prayed for victory. During the first three weeks she seemed to be able to overcome a number of her sins, yet there was one sin that she just could not overcome. One day while she was playing the piano, she stopped and wept. After a while, I asked her what her trouble was. She replied, "It is impossible. In this matter, I am helpless. During these weeks I have been dealing with my sins every day. Many sins I have overcome, but concerning this habit of loving snacks I just am helpless. I am a missionary. I dare not tell this my sin to anybody." As she spoke, she wept. I let her weep, but I was glad in my heart and I even laughed. "Why do you laugh?" she inquired. Then I said to her: "I am so glad that today you have come to the realization that you are not able. Twenty more days have now passed; I thank God that the day has come for you to know that it is impossible for you. You should understand that the Lord has allowed this impossible task, as it were, to remain in your life in order that this may serve as the litmus test of your victory. Let me tell you this: The Lord wants you to see your impossibility. When you realize it is impossible with you, then God will show His possibility to you." Do you see the principle here? Impossible with you, but possible with God.

A mother, a sister in the Lord, was a good woman. She worried about her children from dawn to dusk. She did not realize, however, that worrying was a sin. But one day she saw it and found herself stuck. Formerly she did not really know herself, but then she came into a deeper knowledge of herself. She truly sensed the impossibility to overcome. Many may know the teaching of victory but real victory they do not experience. One of the reasons is due to their shallow knowledge of their own selves.

Not Trying to Do

We have already seen that Christ is our victory; but to let Him be our victory has its condition, and that is, we must first recognize that it is impossible with us. If you insist on saying in your heart that you are able, then Christ cannot live for you nor can He overcome for you. For victory is possible only to those who are completely defeated. Now, here is another problem: "Impossible" is one thing, "Not trying" is another. When is a leper cleansed according to Leviticus chapters 13 and 14? It is when leprosy covers all the skin of him who has the plague from his head even to his feet then he shall be pronounced as clean (see 13.12-13). Recall that our Lord called a dead man to arise, not a half-dead half-living man to arise. We must truly see that apart from Christ we can do nothing. So, the conditions for victory are first, seeing ourselves impossible, and second, ourselves not trying. For impossibility and trying are two different things. Some people know they cannot, but they still try. For example: Here is a weight of one hundred pounds, but you can only lift fifty pounds; yet you insist on trying to lift the hundred-pound weight. This is a vain attitude. God knows that we are so corrupted that to be crucified is the only way for us. Nonetheless, our corruption is so deep that we still want to try. So, we spend much time trying. Such people will never be delivered. "Try not" means that henceforth you not only acknowledge that it is impossible with you but also cease trying to use your own strength. You know that Christ is already living in you and that He will do what is impossible to you. His strength is not used to supplement your lack in work. His life does not serve to mend your hole in life. He desires to live in you and for you. Whenever you exert your own strength, Christ is unable to live for you. Hence, we need to see not only "impossible with us" but also to decide "not trying to do" ourselves.

"Know ye not as to your own selves, that Jesus Christ is in you? unless indeed ye be reprobate" (2 Cor. 13.5b). Whoever has come to the Lord is no longer a reprobate, for he now has Christ in him. Christ is in you, but your old man is also in you. There are now two men in you. With Christ and your old man both living in you, this creates a real problem. What should you do? The problem will be solved if one of the cohabitants moves out. The salvation of God is moving out the old man, having him crucified so that Christ alone remains in you. This is victory.

Once there was a foreign sister living in Yantai. She had three children who frequently annoyed her. She said to me: "I am not able to be patient. What should I do?" I told her this: "If you cannot be patient, then you should not even try to be patient. You just come to the Lord and say: 'O Lord, I am not able to be patient. From now on, I will not even try to be patient. O Lord, You be my patience. I will not try again.'" Let me tell you, if you learn how to let go, if you give up your trying, and if you believe in the ability of the Lord, then you will experience victory all the way. Walking in this victorious way is indeed a glorious path.

Let Go and Commit

Victory comes from your not being anything. You lay down yourself and commit everything to God. You say to Him: "O God, I commit all to You. Henceforth I will not look at myself as to how good or how bad." Once you commit yourself, God will without doubt take you over. You let go, and God takes over. For instance, as I offer a cup of tea to you, the moment I let go my hand, you take it with your hand. Such is always the way. Suppose I offer a cup of tea to you, but I do not let go my hand on the cup; then you are not able to receive it. It is the same way with God. He waits for you to let go before He can take you in His hand. If you wait for God to take you before you let go of yourself, He can do nothing but wait till you let yourself go. For God will never ever do the work of just helping, nor will He ever allow men to help Him. He must do the entire work so that He might have all the glory. If you want to do it yourself, then God will not do anything. You must stop working, then God will begin to work.

In case a temptation comes, you can tell the Lord: "O Lord, here comes a temptation. I am not able to resist, nor will I try to resist. O Lord, will you please go and resist it." If you let go like this, letting Christ do it, He will invariably be your victory. Every day we live, we live by grace.

A certain brother in Tianjin asked me how to let go. I said, "Brother, what is your position in the company?" "I am the head of the cloth and silk department," he replied. So I asked him: "Suppose the owner of your company were to tell you that the board of trustees has decided to lay you off and ask you to be ready for the transfer; what will you do?" "Then I have to prepare for the transfer," he said. I continued by asking: "If after the transfer, an agent came to you trying to convince you to purchase a certain kind of new silk, will you still calculate how much stock you have and how much merchandise you have to purchase for the company?" "No," he replied, "for I will inform the agent that I have resigned and left the company. You will have to contact the new head." So, this is the way to let go. We have been disemployed by God. We do not need to do anything. We should let go and let God do it. When Satan comes to you, his motive is to stir you up so that you will sin. As soon as you are stirred, he has his chance. Our victory depends on our immediately not thinking of a way to resist. The more we resist, the more we fail. Hence, let us boldly put everything in the Lord's hand without any worrying. This is called victory. This is letting go.

One brother said that he fought with sin every day. A young brother told him, "If I were you, I would not fight." He retorted with: "I was defeated, even fighting and resisting; what will happen if I do not fight and resist? Will not the defeat be more serious?" "No," answered the young brother, "I would tell God, 'O God, I cannot. O God, You do it for me. I commit it to You.'" This, then, is the secret of victory. You just let go, and the Lord will take up. Victory relies not on how much you do but on how much God does.

A brother intended to go down a dried-out well. He tied a rope to the opening of the well and then he lowered himself by holding onto the rope. At last he came to the end of the rope. He had no idea how much deeper was the bottom of the well. So he decided to climb back up to the well opening. As he tried to climb, however, he found his strength was almost exhausted. He could neither climb up nor climb down. He cried for help. But this place was deserted and the well was deep. He cried and cried, but no man came to rescue him. He was totally exhausted. Being a Christian, he began to pray: "O God, I pray that at least You will let me fall into eternity." After he finished praying, he let go his hold on the rope and dropped from "heaven to earth." As it turned out, the fall was a mere two or three inches. How regretful he was that he should have held onto the rope and to have struggled so long. He could have let go much earlier. Victory is in letting go! Let go! Do not be afraid. You will not fall into eternity. You will fall upon the Rock of Ages. Let go your hand and you will overcome. Victory comes from Christ, not from you. Let go and let Christ, and it is done. For the life of victory is given to one who lets go completely.

When I was in Yantai, a physician, Dr. Shih, came to hear me preach. He had a history of smoking for more than ten years. Four years ago, he got saved, and he married a sister in the Lord. His wife had studied theology, and was a virtuous woman.

During these four years he tried to quit smoking. One year he stopped smoking seven or eight times, and the longest time of not smoking was four consecutive days. Even when he had no cigarette in his hand, his mind was full of smoke. So he smoked again. He frequently did so in secret, and when he saw people coming, he would snuff out the cigarette and put a Chinese hygienic pill in his mouth. He was afraid people might know he had been smoking. He himself said that during that year he suffered greatly for trying to quit the habit. He tried and tried, but always failed. So, he came to see me, inquiring of me as to what he should do.

I was glad after I heard his story, for here was another person who was going to experience victory. So I asked him: "Brother Shih, you are a physician. Would you admit a healthy person to your hospital?" "No," he replied, "the hospital will not admit the healthy. Only the sick we admit." When I heard this, I was overjoyed because the Lord Jesus was going to have another outpatient. The Lord would have another opportunity to manifest His might. I said to him: "Do you know that the Lord Jesus only takes care of incurable diseases? You say you are unable to quit smoking. Is this an incurable disease?" "Yes indeed," he replied, "I have tried to quit smoking for three or four years already, but I just cannot stop. This truly is an incurable disease to me." Then I said: "Good, now let us see what the Lord Jesus can do. You need to do nothing but to tell the Lord: 'I cannot quit smoking, I am hopeless, and from now on I will not even try again to quit smoking. O Lord, I commit myself to You. O Lord, You are able. Please deliver me.'"

Then I repeated to him the words of Paul in 2 Corinthians 12.9: "He hath said unto me, My grace is sufficient for thee: for my power is made perfect in weakness. Most gladly therefore will I rather glory in my weaknesses, that the power of Christ may rest upon me." And then I said: "You cannot quit smoking; that is a good sign. Paul boasted of his weakness. How did you react to your weakness? Did you shed tears? No; so you should tell the Lord, 'Lord Jesus, I am weak, I have failed to quit smoking, I just cannot quit. I will still always smoke. But, Lord, You are in me. Now I will not even try to quit smoking. You must do it for me.'" So he prayed accordingly and returned home.

The next day he came to tell me what he had spoken to his wife. "For four years you have quarreled with me about smoking and I still continued to smoke. But when I went to God, in five minutes all was solved." "Will you smoke again?" I [Nee] asked. "Why not?" he answered, "I myself will forever smoke. I, Shih, will continue to smoke even after five or ten years more. He who makes me quit smoking is the Lord Jesus." He had truly overcome.

In Yantai, a lady came to see me. I asked her whether she believed she would henceforth live a victorious life. Her reply was that it would take some length of time before she would ever dare to answer such a question. By her words I detected her defeated living. For victory is not proven by long waiting. Victory is believing that regardless the circumstances, the Lord lives in me and for me. Victory comes by one letting go and simply believing. If we fail to overcome, it is either due to our failure in letting go or due to our lack of believing. Otherwise, there will be victory.

To sum up, then, the secret of victory lies in (1) seeing our own impossibility, (2) letting go our hands, (3) seeing the Lord's ability, and (4) having living faith daily, believing that henceforth the Lord is going to live for us. You can believe that He lives for you when you get up joyfully in the morning. You must also trust Him for living in you even if you are not so joyful when you get up. Then your day will always be spent in victory and glory. Never forget to commit yourself to the Lord, putting yourself in His hand, and then believe that He has already taken you over and will live out the victorious life in you. You are not testing whether it works; instead, you are fully committed and absolutely believing. As you commit, the Lord works. Believe in your heart and the Lord will not fail to live for you. You will live a victorious life if you do not fail in letting go and believing.[*]

---

[*] Note: Message given at Fuzhou, Dec. 20, 1936.

Chapter 6

HOW TO EXPERIENCE
THE VICTORIOUS LIFE (2)

We have already seen that having Christ living in us is having the victorious life. The condition for victory is quite simple. If we retreat, resign, step aside and let go, Christ will manifest His victory in us. Without letting go ourselves, we will never be truly victorious. So, we must continue to consider this matter of how to let go and how to commit.

Let Go

When I was in Yantai, a sister in the Lord told me that she had tried but failed, and that she did not really know how to let go of herself. I asked her whether she had ever ridden in a car while visiting friends. Her answer was positive. I further asked, if there was any occasion when as she arrived at her friend's home and before she could pay the fare, her friend had come outside and paid it for her. So she said yes and added that she had tried to pay the fare back, but her friend returned it to her. So I further illustrated the point to her: "Suppose the fare she had paid for you was twenty cents and the driver had taken it and departed. Yet you do not want her to spend that kind of money for you; so, upon your taking leave, you suddenly thrust twenty cents into her hand. You and your friend strive against each other. Finally, you leave the money on the road and walk away. But you think in your heart, Will my friend pick the money up? Suppose she does not; then a passerby may pick it up. So you quickly turn your head and take a quick glance. You see that she has not picked up the money. Yet you walk away a few more steps and cast a look back at it once again. Let me tell you, with your casting a glance back, your friend will never pick it up. But if you lay the money down on the road, walk away without casting a backward glance, most likely your friend will pick the money up." After I used this illustration, she began to understand and thereby entered into the victorious life.

I made mention before of the lady who loved to snack. Before my conversation with her, she had invited people to a meal that was to occur a few days afterwards. When that day came, during the kmeal she suddenly cried because she realized she had not overcome; she was yet defeated because she had not let herself go. "Let go and go home" runs a Chinese proverb. As a person lets go, God will take over. Yet we always try to find the way out. While God has already judged us as hopeless, He asks nothing from us except a letting go of our hands. For as long as we are thinking of doing something, God will let us try. Until one day, you say: "O Lord, I thank You. I can do nothing, but I believe You can." And as you so trust God, you will immediately see Him working. Many commit themselves to God on the one hand but on the other hand feel uncomfortable; and hence, they look back wondering if God *will* take over. This is not real commitment. God insists on taking full responsibility. If *you* are still in charge, He will not do anything. He will wait till you truly let go and cease worrying after you have committed yourself to Him. You cease worrying what will happen to you, whether good or bad. With such kind of commitment, God will certainly take over and be fully responsible. You let go, and He takes over.

Believe

We know that even after letting go, many still suffer defeat. This is because of their unbelief. After letting go, it must be continued with believing. Letting go is negative; there needs to be believing, which is positive. You must believe that you have already overcome. To put it more accurately, believe that the Lord has already lived in you, and that you already have uninterrupted communion with Him. You already have a life of prayer as well as a heart of obedience. You have the power to overcome sins because Christ lives in you. "Let go and believe" is a definite action. Every Christian should know the date and time he made the transaction. It is like knowing the specific date of one's salvation. Letting go and believing is very specific. After it occurs, it must be maintained as such. This is to be continued, not once for all. Some may complain that this will be difficult, for how can we always remember? Immediately after we listen to a sermon, we may indeed remember. But when we are busy with studying or busy with works, we forget. What, then, should we do?

We have a brother in the Lord who is in charge of a factory. He confessed that during office time, he was frequently deafened by the noise of the machines. He wondered how he could always be in Christ. So I asked him, "When you forget that you are in Christ, are you still in fact in Him?" He thought for a while and replied, "Indeed, I am still in Christ." Thank the Lord, it matters not whether I remember or forget; the question is, will Christ remember me? I may forget the Lord, but the Lord will never forget me. You and I must see that we are not the problem because we are now in Christ. We can rest in the Lord, for He will bear full responsibility.

Just As I Am

One brother raised the question, "What will happen if I let go today but do not let go tomorrow?" Well, you can go to the Lord and tell Him: "O Lord, I just cannot let go, nor do I intend to let go. Yet thank God, for You are able to make me let go!" Even if you cannot believe, there is still a way out. You may tell the Lord: "O Lord, I cannot believe and I do not intend to believe. But I thank You because You can believe for me." There is no weakness in us that is able to bind God's hand. Come to the Lord just as you are. Nothing is impossible. Hallelujah! After this transaction, you will see how the Lord overcomes for you the sins you cannot conquer yourself.

Another brother inquired that if he lets go and believes today, would he henceforth never sin again? No, you still have the possibility to sin. Yet there will be a great difference before and after your letting go and believing. Before you obtain the secret of a victorious life, your defeat is certain and your victory is seldom. But after the transaction, you may see that victory is certain and defeat is occasional. You now have a note of victory. You will be altogether different. You are able to overcome the sin that always besets you. How very different your life will be.

How to Deal with Temptation

A victorious life is nonetheless exposed to temptation. How do you deal with temptation when it comes? The temptations which Christians meet daily are of two different kinds: one comes slowly, thus allowing time to reflect; whereas the other comes suddenly without providing you time to consider. Because these two kinds of temptation differ in length of time, therefore the ways to deal with them are also different. Let us look at them one by one.

(1) Dealing with Slow Temptation

The way to deal with temptations which come slowly is like crossing the threshold of victory. When temptation comes, you will not face it yourself; instead, you can hide yourself behind the Lord. You do not resist, you do not fight against it; you merely tell God that you would naturally like to lose your temper, that you are not going to be patient yourself. You can say: "Lord, I thank You and I praise You. You be my patience. It is not I myself who is able to overcome. As Your blood has saved me, so Your flesh, that is, Your life, will likewise deliver me." If indeed you stand on such ground, temptation will flee from you. Were you to struggle with temptation, were you to resist it, it would stay with you. But as you say, I cannot, but God can; as you boast of your weakness and boast of the power of God: then the temptation will immediately be over. You have crossed the threshold of victory.

(2) Dealing with Sudden Temptation

Concerning the second kind of temptation, we ought to know that sudden temptation to sin is like a fiery dart. It comes to you unaware. To deal with such fiery dart, we must use faith as a shield. Many treat faith as a pair of tweezers. When the fiery dart comes, we use faith as tweezers to pluck it out. This is a waste of energy. What is a shield? A shield is that which stands between the enemy's fiery dart and you. We must pray daily with faith that God will deliver us from temptation, from encountering the unexpected kind. We must also believe that during the day Christ is able to live out His life in us. We must believe that formerly, while we were in Adam and joined to Adam, we could sin without exerting our will or strength; so now, being in Christ and joined to Him, we also believe that we will have the patience and holiness of Christ manifested in us without our determination. Every morning we rise up believing that God will deliver us from all those sudden temptations. Every morning we arise believing that the life of Christ will live itself out without our consciousness.

Should someone say that he dare not guarantee that he will not fail throughout the day, that person will definitely be defeated. Even the person who declares that he will overcome this day has no guarantee that he will not fail. Victory is only for the one who is able to say: "O Lord, I thank You for telling me that Your grace is sufficient for me. Lord, I am weak and always weak. I have no strength. I cannot overcome sin. But it is You who said that Your grace is sufficient for me. I therefore commit myself to you, I believe in You. I believe Your grace is sufficient." Such a one has the word of the Lord. He believes the Lord's word and stands on it. He shall overcome. The shield of faith needs to be used constantly. How blessed is the Lord's prayer to the Father. He asks the Father to deliver us from temptation (see Matt. 6.13). You, too, must pray the same prayer: "O Lord, deliver me from sudden temptation." You will witness how He delivers you.

How to Deal with Trial

There are also those occasions when we meet not just temptation but also trial. For example, suppose a sister is persecuted by her husband in forbidding her to attend meetings. To deal with such trial likewise requires faith. If this is real gold, it will be manifested as gold under intense fire. It will not be burnt into copper. True faith is long-lived. So, when you encounter any trial, do not be discouraged or draw back. On the contrary, stand firm on the word of God, believing that God will manifest His victory in your life.

When I was in Yantai, a sister in the Lord came to see me. She said to me, "I believed I had crossed the threshold of victory, but my victory was short-lived. It lasted only one week. After that I failed again. What is the matter with me?" I replied with an illustration: Suppose your child is playing at the entrance of your house. A rickshaw man tells him that he was bought by his mother from the pharmacy. Your child runs home and asks you, "Was I born by you or bought by you?" You tell him that he was born by you and that he should not believe a stranger's word. He goes outside again and meets the same person who says to him: "You fool, you are deceived by your mother for you were bought, not born, by your mother. Indeed, I was there when your mother bought you." That richshaw man repeatedly says to your child that he was not born by his mother. The stranger even presented two or three witnesses. So what will your child believe — your word without any evidence or the stranger's lie with seeming proofs? If your child listens to your word, he will stand firm against the lie of the stranger. He will laugh in his heart against the stranger, he will not believe in what the stranger has said even if the latter should lie more. Now this is the way we believe in God's word. We do not need any evidence. Whatever God says is true. My own feeling may be wrong, even my experience can be false. I only believe that God's word is true. Such faith is not fearful of trials.

There was another brother who testified, saying: "I spend many days of my life sitting at the bow of the boat because I have the Lord resting in the stern of the boat. I look down on all temptation and trials." Such is the assurance of a man of faith. However, even this does not guarantee that you will never fail, for the possibility of failure is always there. But as soon as you fail you immediately confess your sin, repent, and ask for the cleansing of the precious blood of the Lord; and immediately you shall walk in the path of victory again. Then shall your victory be from glory to glory.

The Nature of Victory Is Complete, the Experience of Victory Is Progressive

The question is raised — Is victory progressive or complete? Victory is progressive; nevertheless, it is not wrong to also say it is complete. Looking at the matter from the viewpoint of God having lived in you and having overcome sins for you, victory is complete. But looking from the viewpoint of measure, God's fullness varies in degrees. For example, a cup, a bowl, and a water pot may all be filled, though the measure of fullness is different from vessel to vessel. Each believer can overcome only the sin that he knows, he cannot overcome the sin of which he is unconscious. If last year you had no knowledge of a certain sin, you could not speak of overcoming that sin. But this year God's light has shone upon you and caused you to recognize it as sin; then, you may overcome it. As your light gradually increases, so does your victory progress. The victory which a newly saved person has experienced and the victory a Christian with forty or fifty years has experienced are alike in nature, though the measure of victory and the things overcome are vastly different. In order to live a victorious life, one must learn daily what sin is, what are the things that dishonor God. Then will we make progress every day.

I have a friend who is a missionary of the China Inland Mission; she knows what a victorious life in Christ is. She had an older colleague who often disturbed her by spreading much false news about her back to England so that all her fellow workers despised her. My friend, however, was patient with her and still showed her kindness. One day she read 1 Peter 1.22 that says, "Seeing ye have purified your souls in obedience to the truth unto unfeigned love of the brethren, love one another from the heart fervently." God enlightened her to see that not only hate is sin, even not loving the brethren fervently was also sin. So she prayed: "O Lord, You command me to love her, but she is so unlovely. She is not just unlovable, she is fully hateful. Lord, I forgive her, but I cannot love her nor can I love her fervently. I confess my sin." For two or three days she tried to understand this newly discovered sin. One day she fasted and prayed the entire day. Still she could not love her. After a day and a night, she again prayed earnestly. By the next evening, the Lord gave her victory. Now she was able to love her colleague, and love her fervently. She was able to intercede for her. Thank the Lord, a week later, even that colleague who had troubled her so much came also into victory. There are still battles to fight, but those

111

are fights of faith. The way of the world is to fight to win, but the way of the Lord is to win to fight.

There were in Shansi three lady missionaries. Two of these endorsed celibacy, and the other one was engaged to a man in England. One day this engaged lady was praying in her room. She felt so lonely that she wept sorrowfully. One of the other two missionary ladies happened to pass by and saw her weeping. She then told the third missionary: "So far as weeping is concerned, we two should be the ones weeping. This one is engaged to a man who writes her often; why then should she weep?" Later on, those two celibates were affected and began to cry for their own loneliness. One day the Lord reminded one of them: "I am with you always, even unto the end of the world" (Matt. 28.20b). And the other celibate read the word in Psalm 16.11 which says: "Thou wilt show me the path of life: in thy presence is fullness of joy; In thy right hand there are pleasures for evermore." They began to realize that this feeling of loneliness was a new sin. Hence, they prayed: "O Lord, forgive us. You are with us, and yet we feel lonely. This is a sin." Thereafter these two celibate sisters lived victoriously. For in the following seven years, they never once cried out of feeling lonely.

Another sister had five children. She was fine in other matters but she always worried for her children. At first she considered such worrying was legitimate; she therefore had no way to overcome worrying. One day the Lord enlightened her, causing her to realize that worry is a sin. With this understanding, she finally gained the victory over worry. With Christ living in you, your victory is measured by the knowledge of sin.

Once I was so ill-treated by a particular person that I spoke a few nasty words to him. But the Lord pointed out this sin to me and required me to apologize. I thought to myself, "This man sinned against me, but I do not hate him, I have forgiven him. Yet the Lord wants me to apologize to him. This I simply cannot do." Every time the Lord spoke, He would not step back. For if His hand touches a point, He will not take it back. I searched the Bible and I prayed. One day I read, "Love your enemies" (Matt. 5.44a). Actually I had already written a letter of apology, but I saw that I did not love him. So, I did not mail the letter. I prayed to God: "O God, unless You cause me to love him, I can never love him." That day I truly acknowledged my impossibility and God's possibility. On that very day I truly could love this brother from my heart. This matter was finally solved after two months. So, the next day I sent the letter to him.

A sister loved tidiness. She could clean up her house but she was untidy with her closet. Two months earlier she testified that one day the Lord told her that she should tidy up her closet, so as to glorify God. So, she began to rearrange her closet. When I heard this testimony, I was deeply touched. The Lord immediately convicted me: "You have never folded your bedding. Will that glorify me?" So, I began to fold my bedding. I had never folded bedding before, but from that day onward, I have done it. I have done it for two months now. Thank and praise the Lord.

The victory in Christ cannot be improved in nature because it is complete, though its scope and measure can be increased. The more light a person receives, the more progress he makes. Less light, less progress. The more one confesses, the more supply he receives from God. The less confession, the less God's supply. If we confess daily before God — "I cannot and do not intend to try, but God can" — and if we believe daily that God lives in us as our victory, then we will advance daily. Hallelujah! On the one hand, victory is complete, for Christ does it; on the other hand, victory is progressive, because as our light increases, our measure of victory also increases.[*]

---

[*] Note: Message given at Fuzhou, Dec. 21, 1936.

Chapter 7

BEARING OUR CROSS

"He said unto all, If any man would come after me, let him deny himself, and take up his cross daily, and follow me. For whosoever would save his life shall lose it; but whosoever shall lose his life for my sake, the same shall save it" (Luke 9.23-24).

"That I may know him, and the power of his resurrection, and the fellowship of his sufferings, becoming conformed unto his death" (Phil. 3.10).

The Objective and Subjective Aspects of God's Salvation

God's purpose in creating man is not simply that man may be fruitful and multiply and replenish the earth; He also desires to have many sons who have His life. This kind of man not only has, externally, the likeness of God but also, internally, the life of God. In the garden of Eden there was in the beginning only one thing yet to be done, and that was for Adam to receive God's life so that God's purpose might be fulfilled. After the fall of Adam, however, God must do two things: first, deal with sin, and second, deal with man. God deals with sin in order that man will cease to be a sinner, He deals with man so that man will not be just man. For the sinner and the man must also receive the grace of God. The sinner needs God's grace that he might have his sins forgiven; the man also needs God's grace that he might have the life of God. Adam needs God's grace both in the garden of Eden and outside the garden.

God has not just objective salvation. He also has subjective salvation. The Passover blood represents objective salvation, while the Passover Lamb speaks of a subjective salvation. The children of Israel, both the young and the old, must apply the blood and eat the flesh of the lamb. Our Lord used this simple type to teach us the objective and the subjective aspects of salvation. The applying of the blood shows us the objective side of salvation while the eating of the flesh teaches us we must decrease and the Lord must increase day by day. This latter is the subjective side of salvation.

We will now proceed with this matter of bearing the cross. Let me illustrate with a chart:

Objective Salvation			
		Provision	**Result**
Dealing with the **Sinner**	Sins (the products)	The Blood	Substitution
Represented by the Passover Blood	The Old Man (the factory)	The Cross	Identification

Subjective Salvation			
		Provision	**Result**
Dealing with **Man**	God's Life (positive)	Christ's Flesh	Release
Represented by the Passover Flesh	Man's Life (common, natural life) (negative)	Our Crosses	Loss

Blood and Cross of Christ
Solve Problems of Sin and Old Man

Let us first look at the sinners in which are found sin and the old man. Sin can be likened to the product of a factory and the old man is like the factory itself. Due to the fallen nature of the old man, whatever comes out of him is sinful. What the old man produces cannot be any better than sin. The Lord's blood is shed for dealing with man's products, that is, to cleanse us of our sins and give us eternal redemption. The effect of washing sins away is two-fold: first, it washes before God, and second, it washes in man. It cancels man's crime before God and gives man forgiveness of sins as well as it cleanses his conscience. The blood does not cleanse man's heart, but it does cleanse his conscience. Our Lord has shed His blood on the cross, sin has been judged, and God is able to forgive man's sin. This is most just. This gives man peace and takes away his worry about sin. In the Old Testament period a leper who was cleansed had the priest sprinkle the blood seven times towards the sanctuary as well as sprinkle the blood onto the leper's cleansed body (see Lev. 4.6; 14.7, 19). This typifies how sin is forgiven before God and peace comes to man.

Blood cannot cleanse our old man — our self with its sin, lusts and passions. In the entire Bible, there is not written once that blood can wash the old man clean. The old man needs to be crucified and canceled. Apart from death there is no other way to deal with the old man. God has no other way to deal with the old man except ending him on the cross. Therefore, the cross of Christ is for dealing with the old man. Whereas the sins of the sinner are dealt with by the blood, the old man of the sinner is being dealt with by the cross. Blood is the substitutionary death of Christ: how He became our substitute and suffered God's judgment for us that our sins might be forgiven. The cross is the identifying death of Christ — in that He took our old man to be crucified with Him, thus concluding the old man.

The Flesh of Christ and Our Cross

So far as man's side is concerned, there are also two aspects: on the one hand, in man there is a positive lack, which is, the lack of the life of God; and on the other hand, there is the unnatural, earthly life in man that is, negatively, in need of conclusion. The way which God uses to enable man to have His life is to give us Christ's flesh to eat. The flesh of our Lord represents His life-releasing death. The Lord's flesh is similar to the fruit of the tree of life. Both flesh and fruit are eatable: fruit is the edible part of a tree and flesh is the edible part of an animal. Hence, by eating the Lord's flesh, we regain what Adam had forfeited in the garden of Eden.

Blood represents the substitutionary death of Christ, the cross stands for the identificatory death of Christ; flesh, on the other hand, represents the life-releasing death of Christ. This last is to give man new life, God's life. But how do we let Christ's flesh, which is God's life, live in us? This is through the practical outworking of the cross — that is, through our bearing the cross. Bearing the cross shows that we have accepted God's work and that we are willing to lose our soul life, our natural life, so that henceforth Christ shall live in us.

In the Bible, the man after Adam sinned is called the "old man," while the man before Adam sinned is called "man." When God crucified you with Christ, He crucified your old man, not your "man." Your hands, feet, brain, will, feeling are all still there. Your personality, yourself, your natural man remains intact. This is how Galatians 2.20 can be explained, which reads: "I have been crucified with Christ, and it is no longer I that live, but Christ living in me; and that life which I now live in the flesh I live in faith, the faith which is in the Son of God, who loved me and gave himself up for me." In this verse there are two different "I"s being used: one is the "I" of the old man, the other is the "I" of the personality — the man as a person. The first two mentions of "I" refer to the old man "I"; the last two refer to the man as a person. The old man "I" is dealt with through our being co-crucified with Christ, and the "I" the person is being dealt with by our bearing the cross.

The Two Sides of the Cross

Our natural life, the animated life of man, is an earthly, animal life. When Adam was in the garden of Eden and before he sinned, his life was the earthly life, without the life of God in him. Hence, this natural life still needs to be dealt with. God's life will be confined in human flesh unless this animal life undergoes deeper dealing. When our Lord Jesus was on earth, God's life within Him was enclosed in the body given by Mary, so that it could not be released. Due to the fact of His dealing with Jesus' human, earthly life, the life of God was able to be manifested. In like manner, such dealings with the earthly life and the old man in us require the workings of the cross. Are these two dealings the same? No, they are different. For in the first instance, it involves the cross of Christ, that is, Christ was crucified for the sake of dealing with the sinful "I." This is an accomplished fact. In the second instance, it is *your* cross, for it is you who bears the cross. This latter instance serves the purpose of dealing with your natural self and it is a daily affair.

Take Up Our Cross

Every part in the Bible has its definite purpose. For example, a chair. If you turn the chair upside down, no one can sit on it. This is why we must place the two sides of the cross in their proper positions. Concerning the cross of Christ, it requires faith: believe and it is done. Christ's cross aims at dealing with sin itself. *My* cross, however, demands obedience, not faith: its purpose is to deal with the self prior to sin; for this "self" can only be dealt with through obedience.

For the sake of helping people, I will mention one thing. And here, I am not judging people, for I would rather judge myself. When you are with a certain person, you may like him, for his speech is sweet without any taint of sin or uncleanness. But you cannot sense God in him. He may even mention things of God, but it only makes you feel that though he is very clean he does not reveal God to you. This is because all these qualities about him come from the earthly life. Mighty in words and in deeds and with good nature — all these qualities are natural; they do not come from the life of God. The natural life is the life which you receive from your parents when you are born. It is the life which remains in you even after the sinful life has been dealt with. This natural life, the old man's life, is able to enclose the life of God to the extent of preventing it from being released.

The Lord spoke the following as recorded in Luke 9.23: "If any man will come after me [which means if any man wants to live the kind of life as He has lived on earth], let him deny himself, and take up his cross daily, and follow me." Immediately following these words He added: "For whosoever would save his life shall lose it; but whosoever shall lose his life for my sake, the same shall save it" (v.24). The "for" at the beginning of verse 24 indicates that this verse explains verse 23. The "life" here refers to "soul life." We all want to preserve our "soul life" — that is, our "animal life," our "natural life" — for such life includes our natural good temperament, excellence and virtues.

The Practical Cross

The Lord wants man to bear his cross daily for the sake of daily cutting off his soul life. How does the Lord bring this about? He allows you to encounter misunderstandings. In such situations you think that you can reason it out. To reason is not sinful. The natural life always likes to reason. Yet here a Christian must learn a lesson. Instead of reasoning he should tell the Lord: "O God, I thank you, when people misunderstand me, how eagerly I want to explain myself. Yet vengeance belongs to You, so I will not seek for understanding by myself." Should you ignore yourself and allow yourself to be misunderstood, and even if you have opportunity to explain yourself, your capacity will be enlarged and the life of God will be manifested more and more. The daily cross will reduce your self life day by day. We all hope to be understood and appreciated, yet God allows us to encounter adversity in order to cut us off. Some hope your children will not make noises so that you can quietly read the Bible. How good that will be. However, if you can endure their noises, you truly are bearing the cross.

Once a father and son came to see me. They suffered so much oppression that they sought for sympathy. I told them that what they complained about was all very real. They were righteous and they had not sinned. But was it a bearing of the cross by so complaining? Please remember that the day you stop bearing the cross, you cease growing. You may still look good before men, even able to serve, but you have already lost the opportunity to grow before God.

When your desire fails to be fulfilled, you are truly frustrated. When that happens, you will resist, disagree, and even murmur. But if you can stop at once and lift up your head and say to God, "O God, I thank You, for this is Your good pleasure"; then you shall notice that your capacity is increased. Without the cross all spiritual blessings will stop. When you are in your home, every time you hear unpleasant words, see ugly gestures, and face rugged situations, you may shed tears and cry, saying to the Lord, "O Lord, I am satisfied, and I accept what You allow to happen to me." By this kind of attitude you will grow up again. Madame Guyon once said, "O Lord, I will kiss the rod that You use to whip me." Miss Margaret E. Barber wrote in one of her poems: "Though my heart aches, I will yet praise You." This is written by one who really knew God and knew the cross.

The Lord will strip away many untouched things in our life. When the cross ceases to work in us, growth and victory, too, are stopped. We as human beings all try to preserve ourselves. Making use of cross-bearing will cause us to lose ourselves, even our soul life. How can we be a blessing to others? Not by how much we keep of our soul life, but by how much we lose of it. The more we lose our soul life, the more we become a blessing to others.

Mr. Charles E. Cowman was a man who knew the Lord deeply. He had served God both in China and in India. Once the Lord opened his eyes to see that if he wanted to be a servant to all, even to be the heel in the Body of Christ, he must joyfully accept all the rubbish poured on his own body. The suffering of the cross is a refusing to taste the wine mingled with gall (see Matt. 27.34; Mark 15.23). The suffering of the cross is exhibited in our not resisting the deep pains in feeling. Once people attacked me by spreading lies against me. My natural life could not stand it. I prayed, "O Lord, is it good enough if I do not resist and keep quiet?" Then the Lord showed me the word in Matthew 5.12: "Rejoice, and be exceeding glad." He meant by this that I must *gladly* accept, not merely be non-resistant.

The Note of Victory

Victory has its note, and it is that of praise and thanks. Should you lose that note of thanks and praise, you have forfeited victory. If you are truly one who is bearing the cross, you will be the person who offers up thanks and praises. There are two different kinds of thanks and praises. One kind — by comparison — is cheap, for you thank and praise God in receiving His grace. The other kind is costly, for thanks and praises burst out in times of experiencing the cross. This kind of thanks and praise is more excellent. This is offering the sacrifice of thanks and praises. A sacrifice is costly because you lose yourself. How many times we need to oppose our own selves and agree with our brothers, or even our enemies. The hardest dealing of the cross is to lay aside your personal opinion and idea, and also allow yourself to fail to get what you desire and like. If you can overcome your natural, animal life, you will obtain God's life. The more you lose, the more you gain. By losing your soul life day after day, you walk day by day along the road of glory. You should accept the lashes of the cross as something joyful.

The Result of Victory Is the Ability to Bear the Cross

Please note that the result of victory is enabling you to bear the cross. Should you be a person who is void of your own opinion, you will be the easiest person to be oppressed. Your wife, or husband, or teacher, or student, or servant or master will oppress you in many ways. Yet remember that nothing happens to you by chance. You should realize that all these acts of oppression are the crosses God gives or allows to you. All who are able to see God's hand in having arranged their circumstances are the most blessed of God. All who avoid the cross are people who love themselves. They fail to recognize the hand of God, thus missing many blessings. Formerly you were not able to face the cross because you lacked the power. Now, thank God, you have the strength to face the cross.

May you learn to know yourself, to know what sin is. If you want to walk in God's will, you have to stand with your oppressor. Learn to love your enemy, pray for those who curse you, break your own self, and learn about faith. Just believe and then obey. Learn not to struggle in circumstances, learn to obey God's arrangements. To others, those circumstances might be adverse; but to you, all such are positive.

Some years ago I read a story. It gave me much encouragement. The events in the story happened in West Asia. A general rebelled against his king and attempted to get the throne. So the king led his bodyguard to fight against the rebel general. He had only three thousand men to fight against a rebel army of a hundred thousand men. When the king saw the general, he tried to persuade the latter to return to him. So the general asked him, How many soldiers do you have; do you know how many I have? The king without answering him spoke to one of his bodyguards, declaring: Jump from the mountain. That bodyguard immediately followed orders and jumped. The king said to another bodyguard, Leap into the water, and the bodyguard did so at once. Then the king spoke to the third bodyguard, Pull out your sword and thrust it through your heart. That bodyguard, too, followed orders. Then the rebel general was greatly frightened and asked the king, How many of your soldiers are like these? The king replied, All of them are like these men. The general dared not rebel any longer, but submitted himself to the king.

Our God also demands that we should ask nothing for ourselves. He wants us to be obedient to the extent of willing to lose our own selves, willing to be trampled upon. Such are those who are cross-bearers, willing to accept all God's arrangements without resistance. If you are such a person, your capacity will be increased continuously and the life of God will flow from you without hindrance.[*]

---

[*] Note: Message given at Fuzhou, Dec. 22, 1936.

Part Three:
Applications

Chapter 1

WASHING FEET (1)

"Now before the feast of the passover, Jesus knowing that his hour was come that he should depart out of this world unto the Father, having loved his own that were in the world, he loved them unto the end. And during supper, the devil having already put into the heart of Judas Iscariot, Simon's son, to betray him, Jesus, knowing that the Father had given all the things into his hands, and that he came forth from God, and goeth unto God, riseth from supper, and layeth aside his garments; and he took a towel, and girded himself. Then he poured water into the basin, and began to wash the disciples' feet, and to wipe them with the towel wherewith he was girded. So he cometh to Simon Peter. He saith unto him, Lord, dost thou wash my feet? Jesus answered and said unto him, What I do thou knowest not now; but thou shalt understand hereafter. Peter saith unto him, Thou shalt never wash my feet. Jesus answered him, If I wash thee not, thou hast no part with me. Simon Peter saith unto him, Lord, not my feet only, but also my hands and my head. Jesus saith to him, He that is bathed needeth not save to wash his feet, but is clean every whit: and ye are clean, but not all. For he knew him that should betray him; therefore said he, Ye are not all clean. So when he had washed their feet, and taken his garments, and sat down again, he said unto them, Know ye what I have done to you? Ye call me, Teacher, and, Lord: and ye say well; for so I am. If I then, the Lord and the Teacher, have washed your feet, ye also ought to wash one another's feet. For I have given you an example, that ye also should do as I have done to you. Verily, verily, I say unto you, A servant is not greater than his lord; neither one that is sent greater than he that sent him. If ye know these things, blessed are ye if ye do them" (John 13.1-17).

The Background of Washing Feet

This chapter in John's Gospel tells the story of the Lord's washing the feet of His disciples as well as His commandment to

127

them that they should wash one another's feet. Let us first inquire as to when the Lord had washed His disciples' feet and had commanded them to wash one another's feet. The Bible carefully narrates the history and background to this situation. So, we shall look at all this verse by verse.

Verse 1a — "Now before the feast of the passover, Jesus knowing that his hour was come that he should depart out of this world unto his Father." This incident of Jesus washing His disciples' feet happened at the feast of the Passover. Jesus knew that the hour of His departure out of the world and of His return to the Father had come. If this evening I would leave the world and return to the Father, what would I do? I would probably return some money to my fellow workers and their wives or I would do some other important things. In any case, I would try to set everything in order. Suppose, however, I know my departure will not happen till five years later; I could very well postpone setting things in order during those years. But since I will soon leave, I must quickly conclude these important affairs. One thing is sure, that whatever things I do, these must be very important, not just some insignificant matters such as asking a child to purchase some candies or to watch a theatrical play. This was true of the Lord as well. Before His leaving the world and returning to the Father, what He did to His students was to wash their feet and ordered them to do likewise. Many last-minute things He did not do; but He did perform this one thing of washing the feet of His disciples. This shows how very important was this matter of washing feet.

Verse 1b — "having loved his own that were in the world, he loved them unto the end." If you do not love anyone in the world, you can let many matters go and not do anything. If you have no relative, no friend, no children, you can simply die in peace. But here the Lord had many whom He loved. If I am leaving the world and I have one whom I love dearly, what I must do as my last act is to leave my last will and testament with him. This is what *we* would do, but the Lord was different. He washed His disciples' feet. He loved those whom He had loved in the world, so He washed their feet. Jesus had a thousand and one things to do, yet He did not do them; instead, He washed His disciples' feet. He did so because of love. Hence, feet washing must be a wonderful thing. If the Lord did not love those of His in the world, this act of washing feet would not be so wonderful. But His love made this act wonderful to us. For it tells us that washing feet is the expression of the Lord's loving to the end.

Verse 2 — "And during supper, the devil having already put into the heart of Judas Iscariot, Simon's son, to betray him." This is rather uncommon: a man was going to betray Him but the Lord Jesus already knew it. Here at this hour, He encountered a most unusual and most difficult situation. Suppose a man knew for certain that his house would fall down and yet he could not leave the house — unlike the rich in Shanghai who can move away and build other houses should their present houses collapse. The poor, however, cannot move away. Or suppose that a war, a most dangerous war, breaks out and you know that within five minutes danger will come: either a cannon shell will come upon the house or the enemy will come. Can you calmly wash your face at that moment? Or brush your shoes? Of course not. We would not engage in such mundane activities. We would do only the most essential things. Yet, at such a critical moment, the Lord began to wash the feet of the disciples. What did this indicate? Would you not think that He did the wrong thing? But no, feet washing here signified something highly important, because the Lord did it at the moment when He knew about the betrayal of Judas.

Verse 3a — "Jesus, knowing that the Father had given all things into his hands." This indicates that Jesus would soon be highly exalted, receiving glory, authority, honor, and the throne. The Lord knew these things would soon happen. Suppose you know you will soon be exalted and glorified, having power and honor. What will you do next? Most likely you will do something which is in agreement with your future identity and position. The Lord, though, knowing of His soon leaving the world and knowing of all the exalted things to be given Him by the Father, washed His disciples' feet. At this moment, feet-washing in the eyes of the Lord is the most important matter. He not only washed the disciples' feet but also commanded them to wash one another's feet. For this reason, we cannot neglect this important passage in the Bible.

Before we deal with the main subject, we must first be clear under what circumstances this feet-washing event had happened.

We have already seen that this occurred at the time of the Lord's soon leaving the world and returning to the Father. He loved those who were His and He loved them to the end. He also knew that there was already danger, for He knew Judas was going to betray Him. But He also was aware that the Father had given all things to Him. It was under these various circumstances that He arose to wash His disciples' feet and commanded them to do the same.

The Meaning of Washing Feet

Let us now see what is the meaning of feet washing. We know that the feet are in constant touch with the earth. The hands may not touch the earth, the head can be high up above the earth, and the back needs not to lie on the earth, but feet must of necessity be in touch with the earth. It can truly be said that if you want to live you have to touch the earth, for you live on earth. The head is for thinking, the hands are for doing, the heart is for loving, the legs are for walking, the back is for resting; but the feet are for touching the earth. Here the Lord did not wash hands. The Jews always washed their hands before meals, but here the Lord is seen washing the disciples' feet during the meal. The Lord did not wash head, back or hands but He washed feet. Why was it so? Here is a rather deep meaning which I hope I can explain well enough for your understanding.

While men live on earth, they are separated from God because of sin. But now this problem has been solved through the shedding of the precious blood of the Lord Jesus on the cross. The sins that we committed in the past have all been washed clean. After we are saved and become saints, we may overcome the power of sin because of the victorious life of Christ in us. The judgment of former sins has been solved by the cross, and the power of sin is overcome today by the indwelling victorious life of Christ. So we would inquire, is there nonetheless anything apart from sin that can still separate from God? Honest people will acknowledge that besides sin there are still many things which can separate us from God, and all these things are related to the world and come from contacting the world.

For instance, in the morning you have a quiet time before God in prayer and reading the Bible. You sense sweetness in prayer and the word of the Lord seems to speak to you. You feel that heaven seems to be so near that your hands could touch it. This happens from five to seven o'clock in the morning. After eight o'clock, many daily things begin to make you busy. Some of you go to trading, some of you go to teach, some go to the office, some go to study, some to medical practice, some to the market, and some of you clean the house and wash the laundry. Each and every one of us has many things to do. But a problem now arises. During the morning, as you pray and read the Bible, you feel yourself near to heaven. But now you go to trade, or go to the office, and everything you are engaged in is legitimate. You have not committed any crime. Yet after three or six busy hours, when evening comes, do you still feel as close to heaven as you did in the morning hour? Sadly, the answer is no.

The student studies at school, and the housewife works at home. After you have done your work, you frequently sense that heaven has backed away and is not as near as in the early morning. You may still have time to pray, but you do not have much to say. You may still be able to touch the letter of the word, but you fail to touch its inner reality. If you attend the prayer meeting in the evening, you want to pray, but you have no word within you. Even though you may come up with some words, yet you feel uneasy in your conscience. You may even shout Hallelujah, and the words and sound may be the same as before, but the meaning and the taste are different. You feel as if there is something standing in the way between you and God. You cannot find out what sin you may have committed, and even if you confess your sin it does not seem to help. If you are separated from God because of committing sin, you must deal with it on the basis of the shed blood of the Lord on the cross. But here you have not committed any sin; nevertheless, you feel somewhat gloomy within. You have lost your former brightness. Such condition requires a different treatment. For this is different from ordinary sinning. The way of dealing with this kind of situation is feet washing. So, what is washing feet? Feet washing deals with something other than sin and yet something that separates one from God.

In our experience, we often meet such situations. Even though we have not sinned, yet we cannot touch God. It is reasonable to us if we sin and are separated from God. But if we have not sinned and yet we cannot touch Him, this puzzles us. Thank God, our Lord not only washes away our sins, He also washes our feet. It is not a washing of hands, for hands point to what you do. You have the authority to do or not to do. It is not a washing of the head. Head signifies your thoughts: you have the authority to think or not to think. It is not washing the back, for you have the authority to lie down to rest or not to lie down. If your head, hands, or back go out of order, you have sinned because these are under your control. But your feet must stand on the ground. This latter is something out of your control. What, then, are the feet? The feet represent contact with family, trade, school, and so forth. All these are unavoidable in daily life. To be a human being, and as long as you and I are still living on earth, we have to stand upon the earth and make contact with it, till one day the Lord shall come and receive us to himself. Immediately before Jacob left the world, he pulled up his feet and rested them in his bed (see Gen. 49.33). What he meant was, Today I have no more need of my feet because I am going to be gathered to my fathers. Before we go to our fathers, our feet must touch the earth, they cannot be withdrawn to the Lord.

In the life of Christians, feet are their unavoidable touch with the world, yet without involving sin. Such contact is not sinful, though it may create some separation between us and God, and thus it causes heaven to be distant and prayer less sweet. As we live on earth, our feet tend to be unclean. We use our feet in standing as well as in sitting. In our whole body, our feet make us feel tired quickly. I do not say our other members of the body never tire us. What I do say is that our feet cause us to be tired most quickly. Likewise, spiritually speaking, our feet often become defiled.

Having understood what feet represent spiritually, we now need to know what unclean feet mean. They must be washed again, even though unclean feet are legitimate, unavoidable, and not sinful. But they cause us to be separated from God or cause us to feel tired spiritually. Such, then, is the result of unclean feet. You may attend a meeting and speak the same old words.

132

Though you may even give a message, yet you feel dull inside. You may read the Bible and seem to understand, but you have no inner response to what the Bible says. This proves that you have unclean feet. Simply put, unclean feet take away freshness in communion with God, while clean feet give fresh, living communion with Him.

Someone once said to me: "Mr. Nee, formerly in Chuanzkou I felt fine, I felt the preciousness of the Lord. But today I have lost my former feeling. I still pray to the Lord. I want to love the Lord, to consecrate myself to Him, and to trust in Him. I have all these spiritual motions, but I must confess that there is within me something missing." This, I say, is dirty or defiled feet. This, for this person, was having his feet defiled through its contact with the world in daily living. Were you to ask him whether he had sinned or not, his answer would be, No. Outwardly he is not different than what he was before, but inwardly the difference is great. He can yet declare that the Lord is precious and that he still loves the Lord, but all this that he says belongs to former years. Currently, how many can say, I love and treasure God's word today as much as former years? Many will say, Last year I felt deeply, but now I do not feel so. This means their feet are tired and defiled! This is spiritual tiredness, a losing of spiritual freshness. For this reason, the Lord says that the feet need washing. So, what is the meaning of washing feet? It means to restore your former feeling, to bring you into freshness of life, to give you new power, thus enabling you to treasure what you treasured before. This is what washing feet is all about. Thank the Lord, He frequently washes our feet.

When we talk, frequently the outer words are the same but the inner feeling is different. Today many believers in Christ cease to grow spiritually. Even their singing, praising and prayers are forced. Such condition can be caused by sin, but many have not sinned. This is because their feet get defiled. This is spiritual lethargy. We ought to know that the Lord wants us to be fresh constantly. Hence, He says He will make us to lie down in green pastures (see Ps. 23.2). There was a brother in Shanghai. He was a laborer and was out of employment for a few months. Two months ago, he got a job. His job was to cut grass. He earned one dollar for every thousand pounds of grass. After these grasses were dried, they would be gathered together into six hundred bundles. Then this dried grass would be delivered to a dairy company. He earned fifty cents per day for delivery. So, he cut, dried and delivered. Last month when I met him, I saw lots of grass being dried. So, I asked him why he was drying the grass. He told me that he did so in order to deliver them to the dairy company. The dairy company would keep them for feeding their cows at winter time. So I said to him that the dairy company used yellow grass to feed the cows, but our Lord used green grass to feed us. The Lord wants us to be fresh. He wants us to be fresh daily. Yellow yesterday, but green today. Yellow in the morning but green in the afternoon. The Lord is the fresh living water, not just water flowing for five minutes. He flows freshly every day, every month, every year. He continues flowing, and not ceasing a minute. He is altogether fresh. But He also wants us to be fresh. Such is the life into which He leads us. This is power, joy, peace and holiness. Only then may we live out the life of Christ. It conquers Jericho, and later conquers Ai. After we have great victories, there are then our daily small victories. This is what we should experience before the Lord every day.

The Bible said that Saul was a head higher than other people (see 1 Sam. 10.23), but God was not pleased with him as king. God had not chosen him as king; instead, God chose David to be king. However, the Bible never said anything about David's head; it only said that he had a lovely countenance (see 1 Sam. 16.12). This means freshness — like that of a newborn baby, a face not full of wrinkles but full of freshness and vitality. For God wants us to be fresh. It is said in Psalm 1 that the blessed man is as a tree planted by brooks of water which gives its fruit in its season and whose leaf fades not (see v.3). We have our leaves which stand for our outward behavior such as patience, gentleness, meekness and other virtues. Whether such outward conduct and virtues are green or are withered yellow or are fresh or aged is a matter of concern. Unless there is the fresh movement of the Holy Spirit in us, these leaves will not be green and fresh but rather will turn to yellow and become old. Perhaps you will get up at five o'clock today as you did yesterday, but today you cannot touch God as you did yesterday. The outward situation remains the same but the inward feeling and freshness are gone.

Why? Because the leaves of your life are dried up. They appear like the things of the old world in Noah's ark, not like the new green olive leaves after the flood had receded. Such people cannot be of great usefulness to the Lord.

A Thirstiness after God

Here I would like to address my fellow laborers. We must know why God puts us in the world today. May I speak frankly that He places us in the world in order that we may create a heart of hunger and thirst after righteousness in sinners and saints. As we go out to serve we must be able to create in men a thirsty heart. In us there should be such an intangible refreshing power and supply that people who meet us cannot help but seek after God. When people are in touch with us, a kind of thirst after God should be produced in them by us. If, though, they see and communicate with us often and yet we fail to create in them a longing for God, this will be our failure. Or if we pray, read the Bible, serve, and preach the gospel and yet we are unable to make people thirsty after God, this too must be considered to be our failure.

Many of us knew Miss Margaret E. Barber. All could testify that she was a wonderful sister. If you went to her and sat before her for a while, you felt something was wrong in you when you left. You began to feel that she had something you did not have. You would begin to desire for that which she had.

Back in 1921, when I was newly saved, I was a very proud person. (As a matter of fact, few are those who are outwardly proud, but many are they who are inwardly proud). I considered myself pretty good by reading one or two chapters of the Bible a day. I went to Miss Barber and listened to her. After I prayed with her a little while, I began to be conscious of my pride, even though she had not scolded me at all. I realized that she had something that I did not have. Now this impact of hers is an example of washing feet. In her presence my feet were washed by her. I had met God. Formerly I lived outside of God, and was old and dark; but as soon as I came into her presence, I received freshness and light. Many times I felt washed clean when I was in her presence. Sometimes, you may converse with another brother; after you leave you sense having been washed. Your spirit is refreshed. You can face God. This is washing feet.

A few days ago I sensed that my feet were defiled. At first I assumed that I had sinned. So, I tried to deal with sin. But God still seemed far away. I sensed a separation between God and me. I did not know what to do. In prayer I secretly laughed at myself that I was being too analytical, for it did not come from within. Later, I went to visit a sister who probably had been saved for only two or three months. She told me how she was saved and how she was persecuted by her family. She expected help from me. After I had heard her out, I told her: "Thank God, when I came here my feet were defiled, but now I am clean because your testimony has washed away my old experience." This is "the renewal of the Holy Spirit" as spoken of in Titus 3.5. It is indeed a most precious word. We need the renewal of the Holy Spirit which gives us spiritual freshness.

A bronze vase needs to be brightened with polish. Lacking such polish, the vase will remain covered with a thin layer of dullness, even though it may not turn green. Likewise, it is possible that we may not sin; yet we are covered with a layer of dullness that shall keep us from shining. The Lord said to Peter, "If I wash thee not, thou hast no part with me" (John 13.8). Why was it so? This "no part with" the Lord does not refer to perdition; rather, it points to having no part in the freshness of communion with the Lord. If we do not have our feet washed, we will be separated from the Lord and will not be able to enjoy the fresh life of the Lord nor have His new supply. For this reason our Lord wants to have our feet washed. We should desire more washings that we may receive more refreshings.

Desire to Wash Others' Feet

There is another side to this matter, which is, we should also desire to wash others' feet. But if we ourselves do not have this victorious life nor the help of the Holy Spirit to enable us to live a life of victory, we will not be able to wash others' feet. Hence, there are those who can wash the feet of others but there are also those who are unable to wash others' feet. It is quite possible that you may live with another person for a whole year, and yet he is unable to wash your feet. It requires a person who is himself living a victorious life before God and is always fresh to be qualified to wash others' feet.

So, then, who needs to have his feet washed? And who should wash others' feet? The Lord tells us: "Ye also ought to wash one another's feet" (John 13.14b). This indicates that all need to wash and be washed. Whoever was spiritually fresh before but now has become dull needs to be washed. All of us need to be washed and be ready to wash another's feet. "If I then, the Lord and the Teacher, have washed your feet, ye also ought to wash one another's feet," said the Lord (John 13.14a-b). In the mutual serving among Christians, nothing is as important and precious as washing feet. "If ye know these things, blessed are ye if ye do them" (John 13.17). I treasure a frequent saying of brother Yu: "Today's Bible is more precious than yesterday's." May we daily experience spiritual freshness. In Darby's translation of Romans 15.32, it reads that Paul was refreshed. This is the result of washing feet.*

---

* Note: Message given at Xiamen, Oct. 10, 1936.

Chapter 2

WASHING FEET (2)

Washing Feet Is Absolutely Needed

Washing feet in Scripture does not merely refer to humility, nor does it mean having daily sins washed. The chief meaning of washing feet points to the maintaining of a constant freshness between us and God. It is absolutely necessary for us to have no separation with Him. We are not able to enter into our chamber, shut the door and pray all day long. We must go outside and make contact with the people and things in the world. Hence our feet cannot but be defiled. Defiled feet is the result of being in touch with the world and thereby inducing a distance between us and God. For this reason, washing feet is absolutely needed. Washing feet has nothing to do with conscience — for conscience is related to sin and sin needs to be washed by the blood. Washing feet is related to spirituality; it is to restore spiritual alertness. It is not necessary for every believer to sin, though every believer does have a time of spiritual dullness. So, each and every one of us needs feet washing to restore our spiritual freshness.

Taking off Shoes Signifies Contact with God's Holiness

Before a man washes his feet, he must first take off his shoes. According to the Scriptures, taking off shoes points to our contact with the holiness of God. When Moses intended to see the vision of the burning bush at Mount Horeb, God said to him, "Draw not nigh hither: put off thy shoes from off thy feet, for the place whereon thou standest is holy ground" (Ex. 3.5). Why did God ask Moses to loose his sandals? Because unless Moses did so, he could not have direct contact with God's holiness. Hence, loosing sandals means having contact with the holiness of God.

Two things separate us from God. One is sin, and this has relationship with the washing away of sin by the Lord's blood.

139

The other is things in the world, and this is related to washing feet. Many today are ignorant of the preciousness of the constant presence of the Lord. Such need first to have their conscience washed by the blood and then be qualified to talk about feet washing. So what we are now considering is directed to those who have their conscience already washed by the blood. Is it not true that oftentimes our conscience has already been dealt with and yet there is still a sense of being separated from God? This is the time for washing feet. Washing feet is for the sake of maintaining sweet fellowship with the Lord. The Lord loved us and loves us to the end. He sacrificed himself, shedding His precious blood to atone for our sins. More than that, due to His great love He comes to wash our feet so that there will be no separation between us and Him, thus enabling us to draw near to this holy God and enjoy His fellowship.

Defiled Feet Refers to Separation from God after Contact with the World

I have noticed several brothers who have the following kind of experience. In the morning as they draw near to God, they enjoy good fellowship with the Lord as though they can touch heaven itself. However, after they go out to work, in the afternoon they can still repeat the words they used in the morning in their intimate fellowship with the Lord, but they do not have that inward taste anymore. All who have walked along the spiritual pathway know the pain of it. Those who have not traveled this way will not understand what we are talking about. There is a way to deal with sin, but it is quite difficult to deal with this other situation. Having feet defiled is not a sin. The Lord has not said that feet ought not be defiled. For He has said, "He that is bathed needeth not save to wash his feet, but is clean every whit" (John 13.10a). For a Christian to sin is abnormal living, but defiled feet is the common lot of Christians because none can avoid it. Separation from God due to defiled feet is not sin but is the result of our legitimate contact with the world. In order to solve such separation, there is the need of washing feet.

"What I do thou knowest not now, but thou shalt understand hereafter"

The Lord purposed to wash the feet of His disciples because He wished His own to continually have His presence. When it came to Peter (Peter had his values as well as his shortcomings: what he did not understand he would not do; what he did not understand, he opened his mouth about and asked), he refused to be washed by the Lord. He asked Him, "Lord, dost thou wash my feet?" The Lord answered, "What I do thou knowest not now, but thou shalt understand hereafter." This verse can be most profitable for us. For today there are many things we have to do that we do not understand, but after a while we will understand. Hence, it is not necessary for us to understand everything before we do or not do anything we do not understand. We need to be humble and flexible, willing to accept God's working in us. It is a blessed thing if we allow the Lord to do in us what we do not understand. Peter said, "Thou shalt never wash my feet." What he meant was, that whether he understood or not, he could not allow the Lord to wash his feet. John especially recorded this incident of the Lord washing Peter's feet in order to acquaint us with spiritual feet washing. We can learn many precious lessons here. For we are often like Peter. What things we do not understand, we will not allow the Lord to do. But if we are obedient, we will let the Lord do them, even those things our brain fails to understand but which we shall know later. Let us be humble and flexible and not be like Peter who stubbornly said, "Thou shalt never wash my feet."

"If I wash thee not, thou hast no part with me"

After Peter finished speaking, the Lord continued by saying: "If I wash thee not, thou hast no part with me" (John 13.8). The Lord said if I do not wash "you"; He did not say if I do not wash "your feet." Why? Because every one who has any part with the Lord has already been washed by Him with His blood. We know that the "wash" here must refer to the feet because the Lord was answering Peter's question which concerned feet washing. So, the Lord's word may have indicated on the one hand that whoever has not been washed by His blood has no part with Him but indicated on the other hand that he who has not received His feet washing is unable to maintain that part with Him. For example: If an electric bulb fails to give light, it is possible that the bulb is broken or that the switch has a problem. So, one will first check the bulb to see if it is broken. If there is no problem there, then he will check the switch to see if some oil has spilled on the copper plate so that it does not conduct electricity anymore. Our relationship with the Lord is of like nature. Oftentimes we think that only serious sin will separate us from the Lord. Actually, a tiny little blockage may separate us from God. Do you have any part with the Lord today? By this question I do not refer to your being saved. It has reference instead to the question of are you continuing in fellowship with the Lord? In the past you had said to the Lord, "Christ is mine"; today, though, are you still able to say the same word? I suppose many will say that the flavor is now different. If we are unable to keep the freshness of our communion with the Lord, then it is proven that we need to have our feet washed. Washing feet is not for possessing outward behavior, morality, godliness, and so forth; rather, it is for preserving the sweetness and freshness of communion with God.

"He that is bathed needeth not save to wash his feet, but is clean every whit"

After Peter heard the Lord saying to him, "If I wash thee not, thou hast no part with me," he changed his attitude by saying: "Lord, not my feet only, but also my hands and my head" (John 13.9). Peter's agreement or opposition is his outside expression. When he agreed, he wanted not just his feet but also head and hands to be washed. But the Lord had already washed his head and hands. These had no need to be washed again; once was enough. But the feet were different. For the feet daily tread on earth, making daily contact with this world, and daily become defiled; therefore, the Lord could not give in to Peter. Hallelujah! Crucified is but once, blood is shed only once. Many want to be saved once again. If so, it would be like what Hebrews 6 says —

that it is impossible to renew again to repentance since this would be crucifying the Lord all over again (see vv.4-6).

I often think about what salvation is. Some time ago, a preacher had a conversation with me. He asked me whether salvation happened once or many times. In reply I asked, "Has the grace of God already been given to you?" "Yes" was his answer. So, I continued asking: "Is the grace of God free or does it require a price?" "Free," he replied. I then asked him to remember two things: first, salvation is free, and free means no cost. No payment is required or requested. Should payment be required, that would be a debt, not a gift. Today, grace requires no payment; but if a payback is asked for later, then grace is a debt, not a free gift. Second, salvation is given. The Jews during the Old Testament period must first have good works and then they get saved. This is more like an exchange. But today we first receive grace and then produce good works. Our salvation — our forgiveness of sins — is free grace; it has nothing to do with our works. Once saved, forever saved. Our sins once washed by the blood of Christ are forever washed away. So, demanding the Lord to forgive your sins the second time would be like what Peter did but will be rejected by the Lord.

In Biblical typology, baptism is done only once — which means that washing of sins is but once. But washing feet is a continuous matter, because our feet need to walk in this world of wilderness all the time. Contamination is unavoidable. Hence, washing feet gives us the joy of salvation continuously.

"Ye also ought to wash one another's feet"

"If I then, the Lord and the Teacher, have washed your feet, ye also ought to wash one another's feet" (John 13.14). On that day, the Lord washed the disciples' feet. Today, He wants us to continue doing what He had done. To wash sin away with the blood is God's doing, but to wash feet with water is man's work. God has not asked us to wash another's body. He gives us water to wash man's feet. We cannot wash another's body because we cannot atone for people's sins, causing them to be saved or to perish. For the work of salvation is the direct work of God. We are only responsible to preach the gospel. On the other hand, today the Lord still washes people's feet; only, He does it indirectly through the washing of feet by His brethren. What is used for washing? The Lord poured water into a basin. What does the water stand for? We know that when the Lord died, out of His side came out blood and water. Blood stands for His atoning death, and water represents His non-atoning death. As blood washes away our sins, so water is the source of our new life. In the Bible, water sometimes means death, but sometimes it points to the life in the Holy Spirit. This life is the new life which we receive when saved. This life comes out of death. Water in the basin refers to the life in the Holy Spirit. We have sins, therefore we need to come to the Lord to receive washing by the blood. But afterwards, if our feet get defiled, we need to go to our brethren to be washed. The Lord commands us to wash one another's feet. This indicates that the work of washing feet must be done by brothers and sisters, that is, by the church. No one can say that he has no need of washing feet. The words "one another" include all the believers. Not only you and I, even Paul and John also need feet washing. As long as we live on earth, all believers' feet can be defiled. This is different from sin after salvation because many saints may overcome sin; but no one in this world can avoid having feet defiled.

How to Wash One Another's Feet

How do we wash one another's feet? For instance, after you finish your day's work, you feel tired. You feel unable to praise the Lord heartily. In the evening, you go to the church meeting. Someone in the meeting asks you to pray. As you pray, you feel unnatural as though your prayer is like composing an essay. You can hardly continue on praying. At that time there may be another brother whose spirit is fresh. His prayer refreshes your spirit as though regaining your spiritual livingness. Now this is washing one another's feet. Oftentimes we come to the meeting and the spirits of all those present are so weak that there is no strength to ascend. Even after one prays and another reads God's word, still there is no reviving. It is because all feet are defiled. There is not even one basin of water to wash feet. Hence all feel depressed. But suppose at that time there is someone present who can wash people's feet. He stands up to pray or to say a few words; immediately, the meeting becomes alive and fresh. Without that basin of water, without that washing of feet, the spirits of all present will remain heavy and downcast. This is also true in family life. Perhaps a brother or a sister comes to your house. After a brief conversation, a little testimony given, all in the family are being brought to God. All the feelings of separation from God are vanished. Such a person is able to wash others' feet and this is precious to the Lord.

We ought to have such an ambition before God, that is, to be able to wash others' feet. In order to do so, we need to have water — that is, to be filled with the Holy Spirit and to maintain constant communion with the Lord. Hence, in our daily life we must live in the Holy Spirit so that we may have living water to wash others' feet. Each time we come to meetings we should have living water to wash other's feet. Never try to wash feet without water, for this will only cause more defilement. Those who are unable to wash feet may still maintain communion with God, but their spirits are definitely cold. Today, the Lord does not wash people's feet directly. He uses us believers to wash one another's feet. Therefore, we need to learn well how to be people who are able to wash others' feet.

"If ye know these things, blessed are ye if ye do them"

In verse 15 the Lord said, "I have given you an example that ye also should do, as I have done to you." The word "as" means "in like manner." What the Lord did, so shall we also do. To do so is blessed. Washing feet is not only a spiritual thing, it also has its outward action. When our Lord washed His disciples' feet, He had a water basin. We, too, must have a water basin. Since the washing by the Lord was a practical washing, we also must have practical washing. In the olden days, our Lord was not just performing; He actually washed with real water. At the time of baptism, there is not only a spiritual meaning involved; for is it not also an outward act of baptizing with real water? This outward act helps to bring out the inward spiritual meaning. Hence, on the one hand we must inwardly maintain its spiritual meaning and on the other hand outwardly use real water. Washing feet is a family affair. It is not to be done in the church meeting. It is like what 1 Timothy 5.10 has said about the widow washing the saints' feet which is something done in the family setting. So, let us follow the example of our Lord by washing saints' feet with water and basin as well as washing them spiritually by refreshing them.

There is another point to be raised here. We must not forget on what occasion the Lord washed His disciples' feet. We know that the feast of Passover is a type of today's breaking of bread. Why is it that our breaking of bread meeting is not fresh and living? It is because we have not washed feet before the feast of Passover. If there are those who are able to bring people to God livingly fresh, then there will be real remembrance of the Lord at the breaking of bread meeting. So, what is the result of washing feet? "If ye know these things, blessed are ye if ye do them." Washing feet is blessed by the Lord. It is well accepted by God and is pleasing to Him. If we do it, we are blessed. May we do according to what the Lord did.[*]

---

[*] Note: Message given at Xiamen, Oct. 15, 1936.

Chapter 3

THE SENTENCE OF DEATH (1)

"We would not have you ignorant, brethren, concerning our affliction which befell us in Asia, that we were weighed down exceedingly, beyond our power, insomuch that we despaired even of life: yea, we ourselves have had the sentence of death within ourselves, that we should not trust in ourselves, but in God who raiseth the dead: who delivered us out of so great a death, and will deliver: on whom we have set our hope that he will also still deliver us" (2 Cor. 1.8-10).

We should know that all the things a Christian receives from God come after regeneration. In regeneration, Christians obtain a new life. For God will never improve the natural life, nor will He repair the old life. Natural and old life belong to the sphere of the working of the cross. God will use the cross to deal with the natural and old life once and for all.

We also know that Esau was an ethical sinner, whereas Jacob was a God-fearing man but who was at the same time a grasping person. He wanted spiritual blessings and God's presence, but all to be acquired in his natural way. He could not lay down himself. His own maneuvering, strength and cleverness never left him. Therefore, God at last had to give him a drastic touch at Peniel. Any dealing which leaves room for a returning to the former state cannot be considered as a drastic dealing.

Jacob sought for blessing, yet he had to flee for his life. He longed to be the firstborn, but he was forced to leave home and his parents. After God touched his thigh at Peniel, he became crippled forever. Thereafter, whenever he moved he was handicapped. The strength of his natural life was thoroughly dealt with by God. Many may receive revelation and light and be dealt with, but such dealings are not powerful enough because the touches of God are not deep enough. We therefore need enlightening from God to show us our natural self to the extent that our original state will never appear again. This alone can be

147

considered drastic dealing, which means that there can be no return.

The Sentence of Death

Death is the way all men will go. As soon as one is born he is traveling towards death. But before death actually comes it may seem that it has no power over him. He may never think of death. Not till the physician notifies him that he has, for example, a case of third stage tuberculosis will he immediately feel "the sentence of death" upon him. This does not mean that death was not present before; it simply suggests that he does not realize that death is as close and so real. Now, though, he knows it and he is weakened by it. In like manner, many know the teaching of the cross, they can even preach on it, yet they are vague in their understanding of the cross. Not until one day God touches them and they have the sentence of death will the cross then become a reality to them. If anyone is touched by God, he invariably will be crippled. For crippling is the sign of being drastically dealt with by Him.

The Word of God and the Light of God

There is a vast difference between the word of God and the light of God. Jacob's leg was crippled because he met God and was touched and dealt by Him. It is in vain if I also learn to be crippled to get the same result. It is like someone who feigns to be crippled; but as he struggles with the crowd to board the bus, he totally forgets that he is crippled. Such is only improvement of behavior, not change of life. A real cripple cannot but limp. Those who can run fast have not been touched by God. Those who pretend crippling are not touched by Him, either. Many among God's children — even among those who minister God's word — are full of mere outward good appearances. Their pulpits are full of teaching, and teaching produces pretension.

I have seen strong people being touched and crippled by God. I believe God is able to touch you. He will take away your self-confidence, causing you not to trust in yourself. This cannot be done by teaching, it comes by the touch of God. It will turn you into a helpless person. This is the sentence of death. There must be once in your life when God must drastically deal with you and give you the sentence of death. This will cause you to confess that all is of God. To deny yourself becomes natural and to pray is easy. One who is truly touched by God needs no reminder. A real cripple may forget his being crippled, but as he takes his first step, he realizes he cannot any longer walk as an ordinary person. Your head may forget you are a cripple, but your leg will never forget its having been crippled. The cross is God's greatest instrument of destruction; for it destroys all that is of the old creation. Such destruction is the work of light. After such drastic work, you will never return to the former natural life.[*]

---

[*] Note: Message given at Hong Kong, Nov. 18, 1941.

Chapter 4

THE SENTENCE OF DEATH (2)

The sentence of death that we mention here does not refer to death itself; rather, it indicates the reality of the work of death in man's life. This kind of death is certain and not avoidable. It causes one not to trust himself again but to look only to God hereafter. Now there are two questions: first, How do I know that I am an enlightened person? And second, how do I ascertain that on a certain day and certain month God has done this kind of work in me? Here we are required to know what is teaching and what is light. If something is taught and it requires you to work it out, that is teaching. Then what is revelation or light? It is when that teaching comes to you and it immediately works in you. For example, your physician tells you that you have a certain disease and he immediately brings you to the operating room to be operated on. The word of God is powerful. If God says let there be light, light there is — it is not that after God says let there be light He commands me to seek for light and work for light. The characteristic of things spiritual is that God says it and the thing is done. We need not worry whether God will do it; we only need to be concerned whether He has spoken. It is not the case that after the ear has heard, the hand will get to work. After Paul was smitten by God's great light, he could ask, "O Lord, what do you want me to do?" God had not preached to him, and yet he could ask such a question. Our many problems lie in what we must do. We cannot find any shortcut. Teaching is no substitute for enlightenment.

The Characteristic of Being Enlightened

A brother from Mongolia came and stayed in Shanghai for eight months. He asked me to lay hands on him and send him out to work for the Lord. I refused to do so. Later he went to Tianjin and wrote a letter describing what he saw and heard in Shanghai. I was quite annoyed and destroyed the letter. I thought in my heart, "What did you know?" It was as though a person who fell from the seventh floor could describe every second of the fall. You immediately knew he was lying. The sign of one who is most deficient in the skill of lying is to say exactly the same words each time. Paul mentioned the same testimony three times, but each description varied because he got confused by the great light. Earlier he would ride on horseback, later he had to be led by others for he had lost his sense of direction. The distinct characteristic of being enlightened is a being puzzled. The greatness of Abraham lay in his not knowing. He had to wait for God's direction. The first thing that happens after spiritual enlightenment is that it makes one wonder what to do. This is just the opposite to the tree of the knowledge of good and evil, for knowledge makes you confident of yourself. Nevertheless, in a state of wonderment, it causes one to trust in God.

Spiritual Reality

Spirituality rests on reality, not on teaching *per se*. Spiritual things do not require mental understanding or worrying. For they rest on facts. All of our problem hinges on the lack of reality. A person who has many questions shows how he is in darkness. He who has light sees clearly. He can see because of the light. After he sees, he has no more question. Without light, many the questions there will be. He will ask what color or shape is a certain thing. But for the person who has seen it, there remains no more question. Spiritual puzzlement carries no doubt. Only teaching will create questions. What we need is one drastic dealing, a one-time enlightenment, one severe dealing of the cross. Only having such sentence of death enables us to truly forsake ourselves and depend on God instead of ourselves.[*]

---

[*] Note: Message given at Hong Kong, Nov. 20, 1941.

Chapter 5

KNOWING CHRIST
AND HIS RESURRECTION POWER

> *"Ye shall receive power, when the Holy Spirit is come upon you: and ye shall be my witnesses both in Jerusalem, and in all Judaea and Samaria, and unto the uttermost part of the earth"* (Acts 1.8).

> *"That I may know him, and the power of his resurrection, and the fellowship of his sufferings, becoming conformed unto his death"* (Phil. 3.10).

The effectiveness of our witnessing for Christ is measured by the amount of our knowing Him. It is absolutely impossible to witness for Christ without any knowledge of Him. As much as we know Christ, so much will be our witness for Him. To know Christ is to know His resurrection power. For in this matter of knowing Christ, knowing the power of His resurrection occupies a principal role. The power of the Holy Spirit is based on resurrection. Without resurrection, there cannot be the power of the Holy Spirit. But with the power of the Holy Spirit and the power of resurrection, we are able to witness for Christ.

Here I would like to ask a fundamental question, Who among us is qualified to be a worker of Christ? Who is worthy to be a witness for Him? Today's question lies in whether one knows Christ, whether one knows of the power of the resurrection of Christ. The power of the Holy Spirit may easily be solved, for it is not the chief objective. As long as we know the power of the resurrection of Christ, the filling of the Holy Spirit naturally follows. For the filling of the Holy Spirit is the result of knowing the resurrection power of Christ. So, let us not seek the filling of the power of the Holy Spirit as our main objective. Although it is good to be filled with the power of the Holy Spirit, we should not make it the purpose of all our pursuit. As long as we know Christ and the power of His resurrection, we shall naturally have a testimony to give and also have the power of witnessing.

Having the Power of the Holy Spirit Is Based on Knowing the Resurrection Power of Christ

Testimony is not a doctrine, a product of much thinking. Testimony is not a matter of theology, it is not simply an interpretation of the gospel according to the Scriptures. To witness for Christ is based on our knowledge of Him. Our witnessing for Christ can never exceed our knowledge of Him. As much as we know Christ, that much we are able to proclaim of Him before God and men. One who does not know the reality of Philippians 3.10 will not possess the power of witnessing as stated in Acts 1.8. This is a fixed rule. Experience Philippians 3.10 and you will automatically have the power of Acts 1.8. Do you know what the power of resurrection is? If you know Christ, you are naturally able to witness for Him and simultaneously you receive the power of the Holy Spirit.

The Condition for Being the Lord's Workman Is Based on Knowing Christ

In Southern Fukien a few young brothers wanted to step out and serve the Lord. I asked them what they would say to the people, what concerning Christ they would say, how much had He done for them, how many times had He worked in them, and how much did they know about Him. Did they know Christ only as Savior and nothing more? If so, then they were disqualified to work for the Lord. Do not even think that because you have a keen mind, therefore you can guide people. What people need is life, not knowledge. What people lack is the Holy Spirit, not the persuasive words of man's wisdom. Since their necessity is life and Spirit, only those who know Christ are able to make people live and cause them to receive life and Spirit.

Today we may wonder, Who is qualified to be the Lord's workman? What are the conditions for being His workman? Frequently we consider eloquence, keen thinking and good exposition of the Scriptures as sufficient qualifications to be a workman for the Lord. We think such a person can serve others, thus he is qualified. However, to be a true workman of Christ, his qualification lies not in eloquence, knowledge and exposition but depends on his history with and experience of the Lord. We should never think that ability to preach and to cause people to repent is sufficient for being the Lord's workman. So, the primary question is, How much does one know the Lord? After you have given a message, how many more messages remain within you? You say you know Christ, and you have proclaimed Him; yet how much of Christ is left in you? It seems to be a common experience that after the Christ one knows is given out there is nothing left inside. After having preached from the pulpit, nothing more of Christ remains. This is shallow spiritual life; such is not the testimony of knowing Christ. Indeed, you know Him as Savior, but aside from this is there yet something more of Him you know? If one has done the Lord's work for a certain period of time and yet he has only one or a few things to share of Christ, such a person is not of much use to the Lord. For knowing Christ as Savior is the basic knowledge of any Christian — it is not any special experience. We need to go on. We must experience what others lack, then we can guide them. What is the use if we only know how to expound the Scriptures and yet lack a deeper knowledge of Christ?

Once a certain brother came to Shanghai. He intended to work for the Lord, but I sent him back. He said to me: "You gave three other brothers the opportunities to speak; please give me also an opportunity. Why should those three be able, and I cannot? You may listen to me, for I can speak as well as those three." I said to him: "Indeed, you are more clever than the other three, you can speak better and you are quite familiar with God's word. People like to hear you. But compared with the other three, you lack one thing. These three men know Christ more than you do. These three have many experiences, but you have only one: your salvation experience. Please bear in mind that it is not in eloquence, ability to preach, familiarity with the Bible, and capability to expound that makes a workman. To be a workman of the Lord is established on the basis of knowing Christ. You may be able to say many things, but those are not bearing witness to Christ. To be a witness of Christ is to tell people of your experiential knowledge of Him."

Here is a pastor preaching. He himself is not born again, yet he tells the people about the doctrine of regeneration. He has been to seminary and there he was educated with many Scriptural doctrines. Thus he is able to preach the doctrine of sinners' salvation. But what this man has is theology, not Christ. When he is asked to speak, he is able to preach many doctrines. But let me ask you, What happens to you when you listen to his preaching? Perhaps you are thinking how good it would be if he were saved. The message he gives is not wrong, but he is unable to testify that Christ is his Savior. Such a person is totally useless in the hand of God.

We cannot say that there is no such danger among us. It is futile for us merely to preach the word of the cross. We must realize that to know the cross of Christ is to know Christ. For what people need is not the doctrine of salvation, but to be saved; not the teaching of victory but a victorious life; not the instruction on meekness, but meekness itself; not the facts of the resurrection of Christ and of His ascension, but the power of His resurrection and ascension. One may speak on the filling of the Holy Spirit, self-denial, self-control, and so forth; but where are the realities of these things? Some can only preach, but others have the experience of what they preach. The one is a theologian whereas the other is a witness of Christ. If all one can do is preach many doctrines without being a witness of Christ, little will be his usefulness.

Suppose a brother comes from the country place. He has not much knowledge and his thinking is not very logical, but he knows how to trust the Lord, and the Lord is his victory. When you converse with him, you may explain to him the context of the text he may quote, you may interpret to him the meaning of type, even instruct him concerning the present truth, instruct him on the meaning of the Hebrew or Greek original, and even on the distinction among law, grace and kingdom. Let me inquire of you, that besides all the words you have given, what else of experience or teaching can you share with him, what additional guidance can you give to your better brother? Perhaps you may even tell him that he must pray in the name of the Lord, pray with faith and with confession. But God may have heard his prayers five or ten times a day, while you who are so familiar with the teaching on prayer and yet your answered prayers in one year are less than his in one day. Do you still think you are more fit to be a worker than he? You know of the doctrines of Christ, but he knows the living Christ, and he has deeper spiritual insight before God than you have.

To be a witness for Christ is based on knowing Christ himself. Without such knowledge one cannot be His witness. This is not to suggest that Bible knowledge, thoughts and speech are wrong or insignificant. These do have their usefulness. But the one thing we must have above all else is to know Christ as our chief pursuit. Whether or not you can speak on the blood is less important than if you have the experience of having your conscience washed by the blood. Whether or not you can speak on the teaching of the cross is insignificant in comparison with how much you have experienced the cross. For we are to be the witnesses of Christ, not the preachers of the doctrines of Christ.

Having a History of Knowing Christ

Knowing Christ involves a definite history. Without such a history, one cannot be sure of having this knowledge of Christ. For when you speak to people on the teaching of bearing the cross, can you tell them of your experience of cross-bearing? When you talk about the power of resurrection, do you have a personal testimony to give about this resurrection power? Or in conversing on humility, have you received that humility which comes from resurrection power instead of that which comes from your old flesh? Or in speaking on patience, can you relate how you were naturally impatient but resurrection power has changed you? You may be able to preach on the doctrines of resurrection and ascension, but do you have a personal knowledge of being far above all earthly things? If you are lacking in these realities you are unfit to share these teachings. For without knowing Christ you are unworthy to be a witness of Him.

During my time in Shanghai many brothers gathered from various places in order to learn how to serve. Many of them thought that after they returned they would be able to preach. They imagined that having learned about such things as meetings, breaking of bread, baptism and laying on of hands, they would be fairly well equipped. After studying God's word a little, they thought they could speak on it. Please realize that such is not the case. For even though you know all doctrines, can you tell people of the things between you and Christ? Can you talk about your experiences of Him? You need to see that only what you experience of Christ can help and supply people's need.

Three hundred years ago there was a well known theologian in Scotland whose name was John Albert Bengel. He received a few students. For those days were different from nowadays. Back then, theologians would accept only a few students. There was one student who studied Paul's Epistle to the Romans with Bengel. Bengel wanted that student to specialize on Romans. One day this student came to Bengel and said to him: "I have found the doctrine on sin in the book of Romans." At that time Bengel was reading a book. When he heard what the student said, he suddenly jumped up and said: "You have found in the book of Romans the doctrine of sin, but have you found in you yourself — in your own life — the fact of sin?" If we do not find sin in our own lives but only find the doctrine of sin in Romans, what effect will this produce when we tell people to hate sin, to deal with sin, and not to trust in the flesh? How can we deliver people from sin if we ourselves have not been set free from the power of sin?

What we seek after is the reality, not the doctrine, of things. Let me tell you a secret. If you hear a man preaching, and if there is nothing following the teaching, you have no need to hear him again. Each time when we stand to speak, we must give people something solid, give them reality and not mere teaching. Only that which is behind the teaching is useful. Teaching alone is not profitable.

Life Out of Death

Paul in Philippians 3.10 said: "That I may know him [Christ], and the power of his resurrection." Why did he not say the power of the cross but said the power of resurrection? Because the cross is death in the negative sense. It is an ending, a terminating. But resurrection is positive. It is life out of death, gain after conclusion. That which comes out of death is no longer the natural life but is resurrection life. For resurrection is what is accomplished through death. Has your eloquence passed through death? Death does not annihilate your mouth so that you can no longer eat; rather, it is resurrection. Have your thoughts been terminated by death and then in resurrection God restores them to you? Does your work depend on you or on resurrection? Your own life is natural, but resurrection life is gained after death. Natural life is given by your parents, but resurrection life comes from God.

What is resurrection? Resurrection is that which comes out of death. Resurrection is accomplished by death and is regained for use. For instance, you have wisdom, eloquence and natural charisma; yet you will say to the Lord: "O Lord, I will not use them, I refuse to take these as my own glory. I would rather die and be resurrected. I am willing to lose these in death and regain them from God's hand." The experience of resurrection is such that you are willing to let all you naturally possess to be concluded by death so that you will no more rely on them, nor consider them as glory. It seems that you have died; your hands, your eloquence and your charisma have all died. What you possessed before is all gone. You are not able to use them anymore nor to live by them any longer (you not knowing for how long — perhaps three days, three months or three years). Now God has come to you. Your eloquence returns to your mouth. Your wisdom comes back and even your charisma reoccurs. However, though in appearance you seem to regain the past possessions, in actuality they are totally different. For all your natural goodness, all which you naturally possessed before are no longer yours. There is a cross that separates them from you. You dare not use them, they are left for the Lord to use. You no longer regard them as your own for they are now the Lord's.

That which was lost in death and regained later is resurrection. This is what is said in Luke 15.24: "this my son was dead, and is alive again; he was lost, and is found." Resurrection is lost and is found. How many of you have been lost? I do not know how many of you would like to step out to work for the Lord. May I frankly ask you, Have you been lost? How much of what you reckon as being useful to the Lord has been lost? Let it be known that all natural goodness cannot be used in work for the Lord. You must lose it in death. Oh, blessed is the loss in death because then you begin to know what resurrection is.

In your daily life, each time you go through death into resurrection, you add one more bit of history to your resurrection experience. Such experience of death and resurrection is cyclical. Through such experience of death and resurrection, all who are in Adam, good or bad, have passed through death and are then regained in Christ. Thus are you placed on resurrection ground. This qualifies you to release the power of the Holy Spirit in you. I love the story of Matthias. Many think that this story is merely to fill in the number of the apostles. The fact is otherwise. For it is recorded in Acts 1 that Judas had forfeited the office of apostleship and went to his own place. So, "of the men therefore that have companied with us all the time that the Lord Jesus went in and went out among us, beginning from the baptism of John, unto the day that he was received up from us, of these must one become a witness with us of his resurrection" (Acts 1.21-22). Time-wise, this means from the beginning of the ministry of the Lord up to His death and resurrection. Out of those who had accompanied the Lord all this time, one was chosen to be a witness with the other apostles. They would not launch out to work at once. They would wait together in Jerusalem that they might receive the power of the Holy Spirit. These apostles could wait in Jerusalem because they had a history with Christ. They had the necessary background. Only those who have a history with Christ and have the right spiritual background can receive the power of the Holy Spirit and thus be able to be witnesses to the resurrection of Christ.

Hence, only those who know Christ and know the power of His resurrection can be witnesses of Christ. Remember well that all who intend to be witnesses of Christ must know what is meant by becoming lost in death and being regained in resurrection. We must have a history with Christ. We must pass through death and resurrection, thus knowing the power of the resurrection of Christ. This alone qualifies us to be witnesses of the Lord. May He have mercy on us.[*]

---

[*] Note: Message given at Xiamen, Oct. 16, 1936.

Chapter 6

THE MIND OF CHRIST JESUS (1)

"Have this mind in you, which was also in Christ Jesus: who, existing in the form of God, counted not the being on an equality with God a thing to be grasped, but emptied himself, taking the form of a servant, being made in the likeness of men; and being found in fashion as a man, he humbled himself, becoming obedient even unto death, yea, the death of the cross. Wherefore also God highly exalted him, and gave unto him the name which is above every name; that in the name of Jesus every knee should bow, of things in heaven and things on earth and things under the earth, and that every tongue should confess that Jesus Christ is Lord, to the glory of God the Father" (Phil. 2.5-11).

The Lord Jesus is God. He existed in the form of God. He had the position of God, and He shared the glory of God. But He emptied himself. He had not emptied himself of the deity of God, though He did empty himself of His glory and position. His equality with God is not something to be grasped after, that is, something to be robbed or forced. For He is eternally equal with God. Yet He voluntarily laid aside His glory and position of God. This is what Paul meant by having the mind of Christ. That mind which was formerly in Christ is now to be in you and me. The mind of Christ Jesus is that while He originally is equal with God, He willingly emptied himself of the glory and the position of God and stood on a lower ground. He did not maintain what were originally His rights but took upon himself that which He should not have taken. This is truly the mind of Christ Jesus.

The Christian life and living is not governed by should or should not. If a person says that people should not treat him in such and such a way, he does not know what the mind of Christ Jesus is. For the mind of Christ Jesus is that even though I am treated unfairly, I can swallow it, yea, I can rejoice in it.

Christ is originally God, yet He laid aside the glory and position of God which was rightfully His and became a man that was below His rank in order to be our Savior. Among the Godhead, there is never such a thing as "grasping."

Willing to Be Defrauded

The guiding principle in the life of the children of God is mercy. For God desires mercy, not sacrifice (see Matt. 9.13). So, a Christian should not expect to be treated fairly, righteously and justly. When people cause you to suffer loss through unrighteous action, will you ask yourself if you can submit from your heart? When people deal with you with unjust attitude and way, are you able to take it and even rejoice in your heart? Only thus will your life grow and will you begin to know what is bearing the cross. Frequently people come to me, saying: "So and so is such and such. Brother Nee, did you know about it?" I would answer, "I know, I know, I know it well." What did I know? I knew your love was short-lived and died. Because "love suffereth long" and "beareth all things" (1 Cor. 13.4, 7).

Today God has not set you up to examine the conduct of your brothers and sisters; rather, He has called you to take up the cross. Each time you cannot take unjust treatment and your heart is full of murmur and rebellion, you miss the opportunity of bearing the cross and glorifying God. Many Christians feel angry at others' faults. The other person is wrong in attitude, but you are wrong in heart. The other person commits wrong first, and you follow suit. Such a person will not be approved by God. What is meant by bearing the cross? When the other person is wrong, you yourself will not be affected by his wrong but are able to keep yourself from being the second wrong person. This is what bearing the cross means.

Humbled Himself

"Who [the Lord Jesus], existing in the form of God, counted not the being on an equality with God a thing to be grasped, but emptied himself, taking the form of a servant, being made in the likeness of men; and being found in fashion as a man, he humbled himself, becoming obedient even unto death, yea, the death of the cross" (Phil. 2.6-8).

162

God's children should have this mind of Christ. Even though among the Godhead there is no distinction of great and small, yet Christ said, "the Father is greater than I" (John 14.28b). Christ puts himself in a humbler and lower place. Hence, we ought to learn how to let our brethren be exalted, honored and respected while we ourselves are being despised and forgotten. What is the mind of Christ Jesus? It is the willingness of losing position and glory just as the Psalmist said to God: "Thou didst cause men to ride over our heads" (Ps. 66.12a). Such a person has no jealousy nor fretfulness. If you can rejoice when another is glorified, this proves that you do not have a jealous heart. Were you to be unhappy in such a circumstance, it is certain that you are thinking of yourself. The issue is whether I can stand to let people esteem my brother higher than I and dare to be inferior to my brother. For such a man knows the cross, and God will soon exalt him: "he that humbleth himself shall be exalted" (Luke 18.14b).

"As to honour, each taking the lead in paying it to the other" (Rom. 12.10b Darby). He who always thinks of treading upon others does not know the cross, nor does he have the mind of Christ Jesus. We must learn before God to dare to let others be honored and glorified while we ourselves may be despised and forgotten. What we lack most is the mind of Christ Jesus. How many of us consider ourselves to be the standard Christian in the world! Doubtless such people neither know the cross nor have the mind of Christ. May God have mercy on us, causing us to learn how to stand on a lower plane and allow others to be higher, loved and exalted over us.

Bearing the Cross

Another thing to be considered is whether we are content to be righteous without having people's acknowledgment and recognition. He who always tries to explain himself does not know the cross. It is enough to be right yourself without the need of others telling you that you *are* right. So long as your own attitude is correct, others' approval or disapproval is not necessary. For the principle of Christian living is not a matter of right or wrong; rather, it is a matter of bearing the cross. This cross-bearing is the only standard to have in our living. So, all we need to ask is, Is this conduct of mine a bearing of the cross? Are we willing to live before God as a meek and lowly person?

The basic principle concerning church government lies not in judging right or wrong. Our standard instead rests on this: that whoever bears the cross is right, and whoever rejects the cross is wrong. Do not emphasize right or wrong; rather, look for cross-bearing. Unquestionably, the cross of Christ is the greatest wrong ever perpetrated in the whole world. There is nothing more unjust than His cross. Jesus Christ, the Son of God, had no sin; yet He was crucified at Calvary. You and I were chief sinners, yet because of Him we need not die nor shed our blood. We received free forgiveness and were saved. Can we therefore not see that this which Jesus endured is the greatest wrong? If we talk about right or wrong, then we need to be crucified. Nothing can be more right than that, for we have sinned and deserved death. For this reason, bearing the cross is an accepting of all the wrongs without mourning or reasoning but with a joyful heart. People of the world may endure, but they cannot be joyful; yet we can joyfully accept unjust treatments.

Forsake All

Another point needs to be made here, which is, that having the mind of Christ Jesus is the forsaking of all. May God give us grace that we be willing to lose everything. Christians should leave room for others to walk through. It can be likened to the trespass offering mentioned in Leviticus: "he shall even restore it in full, and shall add the fifth part more thereto" (v. 6.5b). We need to learn to be defrauded and stamped upon. Christ Jesus had no need to be a bondslave, yet He emptied himself and took upon himself the form of a bondslave; forsaking all that was rightfully His and taking upon himself all that He should not have received. Hopefully, we may hereafter learn to be cheerful under unjust treatment. If it pleases God to put me in such a situation, I will joyfully receive it because bearing the cross is far above all other glories and positions. What, then, is bearing the cross? "Himself he cannot save" (Matt. 27.42b). He who refuses to save himself

— and his glory, especially refusing to save his own feeling — is truly one who bears the cross. God will surely bless such people.[*]

---

[*] Note: Message given at Penang, April 3, 1938.

Chapter 7

THE MIND OF CHRIST JESUS (2)

"Have this mind in you, which was also in Christ Jesus: who, existing in the form of God, counted not the being on an equality with God a thing to be grasped, but emptied himself, taking the form of a servant, being made in the likeness of men" (Phil. 2.5-7).

We will continue meditating on the mind of Christ. First, we shall see how Christ took upon himself the form of a servant or bondslave; and next, we shall see how He was made in the likeness of man.

In these two steps of emptying, the Lord Jesus first of all laid aside the position of God and took up the form of a bondslave. Having become a bondslave, He then stood on the ground that was not of His rank, and accepted all kinds of treatment that was not His due.

Accept Restriction and Forsake Freedom

What is meant by the Lord "being made in the likeness of men"? In order to become man, He was clothed with the flesh and blood of man. He was a man outwardly, yet was God inwardly. He was originally God who is omniscient, omnipotent and omnipresent. He was Spirit who fills the entire universe. But when He came to be man, His Spirit became restricted by a body. The omnipresent God was confined within a body. Where His flesh was, there was the Godhead within. In taking the likeness of man, He suffered the greatest restriction. He was omnipotent, His power was exceedingly great; yet during His days on earth as man, He endured great limitation. Though He did perform many miracles in those days, those miracles were limited by what His human flesh permitted. There were numberless wonders He could perform, yet He was restricted by His fleshly body. He was circumscribed by the weakness of the flesh. He got tired, He must sleep, and He could suffer. He was not free as God. As long as He lived in the flesh, He must obey the laws of the flesh. We enjoy our sleep, but He as the God who never sleeps nor slumbers was now obligated to sleep like you and me. His sleep was a restriction. Not only that, He grew up like an ordinary man from childhood to manhood. The omniscient God could also grow up! As a bondslave our Lord gave up His glory, as a man He gave up His liberty.

We all long to be like the Lord, long to have the mind of Christ Jesus. But are we willing to lay down our glory and freedom? All restrictions, like all deprivations, are spiritually profitable. God gives you a restrained hand so that instead of resisting, you gladly accept restriction. Alas, how people seek for freedom! Yet the restriction which God gives may we not only submit to but even receive with joy. When God gives you a restrained hand and takes away your freedom, He will not give in or relent until and unless you learn the lesson. But as soon as you learn, He will set you free. When the cross comes to you, you will find yourself going away from God if you either flee or reject the cross.

Christians today usually struggle over their environments, trying to shake off the restraints of God and regain their freedom. However, the life of Christ is manifested in these adverse environments. When environments are smooth, this life is unable to reveal its power. For under an adverse environment we naturally tend to rebel; yet because Christ is within, we are willing to forfeit our freedom and accept restriction. It is a bad thing for a Christian not to submit to the providential arrangement of God. We should not resist God's sovereign arrangements of our circumstances. Just as Jesus Christ joyfully accepted restriction, so should we also. Our restricted environment and how we react to it will prove whether we are growing or we have failed. Blessed is he who can praise, not murmur, under restriction! For his heart is in harmony with God.

When the cross comes, it deprives you not only of your glory but also of your freedom. Most Christians today try to bypass the cross in order to lessen their pain. Hence, they lack the mark of the cross in their lives. They grow big and fat. True, they have less pains, but they also have less marks of the cross. It all depends on whether you are willing to hurt yourself for the sake of accomplishing God's will. Our natural life needs to be wounded so as to make real growth. In home, in work or in the church, God gives us restrictions that provide us with opportunities of rubbing off the rough edges of ourselves. Sometimes, God puts some brothers and sisters in the church who can only cause troubles instead of provide helps. We wonder why God would place such people in the church. The purpose is in using them to be our restriction. For this reason, we ought not struggle to be free, because freedom will not build us up. All upbuilding comes from restriction in environment.

David chose for himself five smooth stones out of the brook (see 1 Sam. 17.40a), because the force of these smooth stones was well-balanced. The power was in David's hand, but only these smooth stones could be used to harness David's power. Likewise, God will also use smooth stones. Naturally speaking, you and I are sharp and cutting. God puts you in the church. Then the storm comes. For among the brothers and sisters you all touch and rub against one another. After three to five years, you have been rubbed smooth. During the times of rubbing, how very painful it is. But without rubbing, how can you and they become smooth? Oftentimes you may feel how good it would be without a certain person in the church. Yet without the rubbings of such people how can you become smooth? Alas, many prefer the by-pass. For when the cross comes, they struggle to be freed. The pain decreases, but the God-given lesson is never learned. Whenever God gives you the cross, He wants you to subject yourself to His sovereign rule and be an obedient, unresisting person in order to be one under restriction.

God's Restricted Ones

Madame Guyon came from a family of French nobility. She was a beautiful and titled woman. Many adored her. Yet God laid hold of her. Within two years, she had already learned the lessons God gave her. Not very long thereafter, she was attacked by smallpox. Pomades were sent to her to recover her complexion and to fill up the hollows of the smallpox. Her first impulse was to test the merits of the remedy in her own case. But there was something in her heart which said, "If I would have had thee fair, I would have left thee as thou wert." Listen, then, to what she herself said: "Fearful of offending God by setting myself against the design of His providence, I was obliged to lay aside the remedies which were brought me. I was under the necessity of going into the open air, which made the hallow [hollow] of my face worse. As soon as I was able, I did not hesitate to go into the streets and places where I had been accustomed to go previously in order that my humiliation might triumph in the very places where my unholy pride had been exalted."[†]

It is as though she had prayed: "O God, if it pleases You that I have a spotted face, why should I desire for a smooth face? If You want one to be spotted, I wish I could be rubbed with some medicine that would make my face even more spotted."

See how the most adored beauty in all Paris was willing to forfeit her beauty and become a spotted face in order to obey God. This is knowing God. This is knowing the cross. It was Madame Guyon who also said, "Should God beat me with a rod or whip, I would kiss the hand that beats me." She truly was one who knew the cross and subjected herself totally under the mighty hand of God. Many who are crippled cannot obey God but are rather full of murmurings. How pitiful! But there are others crippled who yield to the sovereign authority of God and gladly accept His will. These know God and know the cross.

I love Job, who said: "Behold, if he slay me, yet I would trust him" (Job 13.15a Darby). He also said this: "He hath hedged up my way that I cannot pass" (Job 19.8a Darby). Thank God, there is a hedge. Even being hedged in limits our freedom, yet it also prevents Satan from crossing God's restriction to attack us further. We therefore need to be those within God's hedge, learning to accept restriction and the lesson of the cross.[*]

[†] Quoted from T. C. Upham, <u>The Life of Madame Guyon</u> (London: Allenson & Co., 1961 reprint), p. 80.
[*] Note: Message given at Penang, April 4, 1938.